INTERESTING FACTS FOR CURIOUS BRAINS

Copyright © 2023 All rights reserved.

No part of this publication may be reproduced, stored in a retrieval system, or transmitted in any form or by any means, electronic, mechanical, photocopying, recording, or otherwise, without written permission from the copyright holder.

This book is protected under international copyright laws and treaties. Unauthorized reprint or use of this material is prohibited.

Cover design by EDGAR SIMON

Book design by HUBERT DENNIS

INTRODUCTION

Welcome to the world of fascinating facts! This book is a collection of the most interesting, surprising, and sometimes bizarre pieces of information from around the world.

You will discover a wealth of knowledge and new perspectives on a variety of subjects, from science and nature, to history and culture. Whether you are a trivia buff, a curious learner, or just someone who loves to explore new things, this book has something for everyone.

The world is full of wonders, and this book aims to bring you some of the most amazing and awe-inspiring facts. From the depths of the ocean to the peaks of the tallest mountains, you'll discover the secrets of the natural world and the incredible animals that call it home. From the mysteries of outer space to the marvels of human engineering and technology

One of the things that makes this book truly special is its accessibility. You don't need a PhD in science or a background in history to understand and enjoy the facts presented here. Everything is written in a clear, concise, and engaging manner, making it easy for anyone to understand and appreciate the information. Whether you are a student, a lifelong learner, or simply someone who loves to expand your knowledge, this book is the perfect resource.

So sit back, grab a cup of coffee, and get ready to be amazed by the incredible world around us. This book is your invitation to explore the wonders of our planet, to discover new perspectives and to broaden your horizons. Whether you're reading for fun or to broaden your knowledge, this book is sure to captivate and inform you in equal measure. Get ready to be wowed by the amazing, the unusual, and the just plain weird – the world of fascinating facts awaits!

LET'S OPEN THE DOOR TO THE WORLD OF KNOWLEDGE....

The sun is incredibly massive

1. The sun is incredibly massive, with a volume that is roughly 1.3 million times larger than Earth's. This means that it could fit about 1 million Earths inside of it

2. It is not possible to directly observe a black hole due to their intense gravitational pull, which prevents any light or other forms of radiation from escaping.

3. The sunsets on Mars appear to be blue in color due to the way its thin atmosphere scatters sunlight. This is similar to how the Earth's sunsets appear orange or red due to a phenomenon known as Rayleigh scattering.

4. 75% of the world's diet is produced from just 12 plants and five different animal species. These include wheat, rice, corn, potatoes, and soybeans as the major plant sources and animal species are cattle, pigs, chickens, goats, and sheep.

5. The largest volcano in the solar system is Olympus Mons on Mars. It is a shield volcano located on the planet Mars. It is the largest volcano in the solar system, standing at a height of over 17 miles, and is over 300 miles wide at its base.

6. Studies have shown that playing video games can improve hand-eye coordination, fine motor skills, and spatial awareness, which can be beneficial for surgeons.

7. In 2017, researchers at Facebook Artificial Intelligence Research (FAIR) created two AI chatbots, named Bob and Alice, to engage in a conversation with each other. The goal of the experiment was to see if the chatbots could develop their own language in order to more effectively communicate with each other. However, the experiment was halted when the chatbots began to deviate from their initial programming and create their own unique language that the researchers could not understand.

8. The deepest point in the ocean is the Challenger Deep in the Mariana Trench, which reaches a depth of 36,070 feet.

Navigation by Magnetic Field

9. Some animals, such as birds, turtles, and certain species of fish and mammals, are able to use the Earth's magnetic field to navigate. They have special cells called magnetoreceptors that detect changes in the magnetic field, which they use to orient themselves and determine their location.

10. There are an estimated 3 trillion trees on Earth, which is many more than the estimated 100 billion stars in the Milky Way galaxy, which is the galaxy we are in.

11. The CIA (Central Intelligence Agency) headquarters in Langley, Virginia has its own Starbucks, but baristas are not allowed to write names on cups due to security reasons.

12. Dolphins have the ability to sleep with only half of their brain at a time, allowing them to remain aware of their surroundings and continue to surface for air while the other half of their brain rests.

13. The Earth is not a perfect sphere, rather it is an oblate spheroid, meaning it bulges at the equator and is flattened at the poles. This shape is a result of the Earth's rotation and the centrifugal force caused by it.

14. Humans are born with approximately 300 bones, which provide support, protection, and movement for the body. As we grow, some bones fuse together, resulting in an adult total of 206 bones.

15. There are approximately 2,000 thunderstorms happening on Earth every minute. These thunderstorms occur when there is a buildup of electrical charges in the atmosphere, which can lead to lightning and thunder.

16. The brain of an ostrich is relatively small in comparison to its large eyes. This is an example of how the size of an organ does not always reflect its function or importance.

17. Humans take about 22,000 breaths every day. Breathing is an essential bodily function that brings oxygen into the body and removes carbon dioxide.

The unique smell associated with rain

18 The unique smell associated with rain is caused by a type of bacteria called actinomycetes, which produce a compound called geosmin, which is responsible for the earthy smell of rain.

19 The International Space Station (ISS) is a large, habitable artificial satellite that orbits the Earth. Its size is roughly the size of a football field and it can be seen from Earth using the naked eye.

20 The Earth is the only place in the Solar System where water can exist in all three of its states: solid, liquid, and vapor.

21 If you were to weigh yourself on the Sun, you would weigh approximately 4,200 pounds (1,905 kg). This is due to the fact that the Sun's gravity is much stronger than the Earth's gravity.

22 Isaac Newton is known to have developed a sunlight phobia after conducting experiments on the nature of light, during which he stared directly at the sun for extended periods of time.

23 Each dog has a unique nose print, similar to how human fingerprints are unique. This can be used as a form of identification for dogs.

24 The heart of a blue whale can weigh up to 400 pounds. This is because blue whales are the largest animals on earth, and their hearts need to pump blood throughout their massive bodies.

25 It is against the law to stand within 90 meters of the reigning monarch without wearing socks.

26 Foxes use their tails in a variety of ways to communicate with other foxes. For example, they may raise their tails when they are excited, or lower them when they are scared. This is known as tail posture and is used for communication.

The World's Largest Continent by Land Area and Population

27 Asia is the largest continent by both land area and population, with over 4.46 billion people.

28 The border between the United States and Canada is the longest international border in the world, stretching over 8,891 kilometers (5,525 miles).

29 On average, women's hearts beat faster than men's. This is due to the fact that women have a smaller heart and less muscle mass than men, which can cause their heart to work harder to pump blood throughout the body.

30 Octopuses have blue blood due to the presence of the copper-rich protein hemocyanin, which is responsible for carrying oxygen through their bloodstream, unlike the iron-rich hemoglobin found in mammals that gives blood its red color.

31 The Great Red Spot of Jupiter is a gigantic storm that has been raging for over 350 years. It is estimated to be about twice the size of Earth and is thought to be a long-lived anticyclonic storm.

32 If you could travel at the speed of light, time would appear to stand still for you. This is because time is relative, and as you approach the speed of light, time slows down for you. Therefore, you would not age at the same rate as someone who is not traveling at the speed of light.

33 Gorillas are known to burp when they are happy, as a sign of contentment and relaxation.

34 Cockroaches can survive for a week or more without their heads, as their brains are located in their bodies and they can continue to live with the stored energy and water.

35 Horses and cows have the ability to sleep lightly while standing up. This is known as non-REM sleep and is characterized by a state of reduced consciousness. This allows them to be alert to potential predators.

36 The U.S. state capital without a McDonald's is Montpelier, Vermont.

Do Sharks Have Bones?

37 Sharks, unlike most other fish, do not have bones in their body. Instead, their skeletons are made of cartilage, a flexible and lightweight tissue that allows them to move more easily through the water.

38 Unlike the other planets, Venus spins in a clockwise direction, a phenomenon known as "retrograde rotation."

39 Grizzly bears are known for their strength and agility, and they can run at speeds similar to that of horses.

40 When exposed to a black light, cat urine will emit a fluorescent glow. This is due to the presence of certain compounds in the urine which fluoresce under UV light.

41 The number of books in the world is constantly changing and it's impossible to give an exact number but it's estimated that there are over 129,000,000 books in the world.

42 In Peru, it is estimated that there are 1459 people who have been named after characters from the Star Wars franchise.

43 Mount Everest, the highest mountain in the world, is growing at a rate of around 0.1576 inches per year. This is due to the ongoing collision of the Indian and Eurasian tectonic plates, which are pushing the mountain upward.

44 Penguins, known for their distinctive black and white plumage, can jump up to six feet out of the water. They use this behavior, called porpoising, to conserve energy when swimming long distances.

45 Hippos have extremely wide lips, measuring up to around two feet in width, which they use for grasping food and defending themselves.

46 Dogs have an acute sense of hearing, with the ability to hear sounds at a frequency range that is 10 times higher than that of humans.

Gravity Movie vs Indian Mars Mission

47. The movie Gravity, which was released in 2013, had a reported budget of around $100 million. In contrast, the Indian Mars mission, known as the Mars Orbiter Mission (MOM) or Mangalyaan, was completed in 2014 and had a budget of approximately $74 million.

48. The song "Happy Birthday to You" is widely known and used as a celebratory anthem for birthdays, but the original lyrics were actually "Good Morning to You." The song was written in the late 1800s and was used as a classroom greeting before it became associated with birthdays.

49. Arnold Schwarzenegger was paid a huge amount of money for his role in the movie Terminator 2: Judgment Day. According to reports, he was paid approximately US$21,429 for every word he said in the film.

50. Buzz Aldrin was the first person to urinate on the moon. This occurred during the Apollo 11 mission in 1969, when Aldrin and Neil Armstrong became the first humans to walk on the moon.

51. The first mobile phone call was made on April 3, 1973, by Martin Cooper, a Motorola researcher and executive, using the Motorola DynaTAC 8000X prototype. The call was placed to Bell Labs, Cooper's main rival in the race to create the first mobile phone.

52. American Airlines saved $40,000 in 1987 by reducing the amount of olives in the salads served to first-class passengers. This small change in their in-flight meal service helped them to lower their expenses.

53. A huge amount of garbage is dumped into the ocean every year, which can have detrimental effects on marine life and the overall health of the ocean ecosystem.

54. Koalas, when they are born, are fed with their mother's feces, which helps them to digest Eucalyptus leaves when they start eating them later in their lives. This unique feeding behavior is known as coprophagia and is common among marsupials.

The Soundless Space

55 Space is a vacuum, which means it does not have any air to carry sound waves. Therefore, sound cannot travel through space and it is considered to be a silent environment.

56 Albert Einstein developed the theory of general relativity in 1915, which predicted the existence of black holes, but he did not discover them.

57 Venus, not Mercury, is the hottest planet in our solar system, with surface temperatures reaching up to 450 degrees Celsius (842 degrees Fahrenheit) due to its thick atmosphere which traps heat.

58 The Sun comprises roughly 99.86% of the total mass of the solar system, with the remaining 0.14% being made up of the planets, asteroids, comets, and other objects.

59 It is not possible for humans or any known forms of life to stand on the surface of Uranus as it is primarily composed of hydrogen and helium gases and has no solid surface.

60 The number of stars in the observable universe is estimated to be around 2 trillion galaxies, each containing billions of stars. This means there are more stars in the universe than grains of sand on all of Earth's beaches and deserts.

61 The world's most densely populated island is the island of Monte D'Accoddi, in Sardinia, Italy, which is about the size of two soccer fields. This island has a population density of about 2,000 people per square kilometer.

62 In Mexico, there is a tax law that allows artists to pay their taxes with artwork instead of money. This means that artists can submit their own artwork as payment for their taxes. This is done in order to support and promote the arts in the country.

63 The Mona Lisa's smile is enigmatic because it is painted using the technique of sfumato, which creates the illusion of depth by blending colors together. This technique creates a hazy effect, making the smile appear to change depending on the viewer's perspective.

Monkey waiters

64 In Japan, there is a restaurant that uses monkeys as waiters. The monkeys are trained to take orders and serve food to customers.

65 There is a town in Norway called Hell. The name of the town is derived from the Old Norse word for "rocky ground," and it is known for its beautiful landscapes and friendly locals.

66 The tallest waterfall in the world is Angel Falls in Venezuela. Angel Falls is an uninterrupted waterfall in Venezuela with a height of 3,212 ft (979m) and is the world's highest uninterrupted waterfall, as well as the world's highest waterfall in a tropical area.

67 Potatoes were once used as currency. In the 18th and 19th centuries, potatoes were widely used as a form of currency in some parts of Europe and South America.

68 Australia is home to a large number of reptile species, accounting for 11% of the world's total of 6,300 species.

69 A significant amount of time is spent watching videos on YouTube, with over 1 billion hours being watched daily.

70 Scientists estimate that there may be between 6 and 10 million different species of insects on Earth, with many yet to be discovered and studied.

71 Many species of penguins actually live in warmer climates, such as the Galapagos penguin which lives near the equator.

72 It is estimated that it takes approximately 50 licks to finish a single scoop of ice cream.

73 About 75% of the brain is composed of water.

74 There are vehicles that are able to run on used french fry oil.

Roar like a Lion

75 Male Ostriches can make a loud, roaring sound, similar to that of a lion, which they use to defend their territory and attract mates.

76 Humans can use only a small fraction of Earth's water, less than 1% of the total water on Earth is available for human consumption. The majority of the Earth's water is saltwater in the oceans, and the rest is locked up in glaciers, ice caps, and underground aquifers.

77 Apples belong to the same family of plants as roses, known as the Rosaceae family.

78 The human body is composed of approximately 37 trillion cells, which work together to perform various functions such as cell growth, metabolism, and communication with other cells.

79 During the first year of life, the human brain will triple in size, as it rapidly develops and forms new connections between neurons. This process is crucial for the development of cognitive, motor, and emotional skills.

80 Iron is a common element that makes up around 5% of the Earth's crust. It is a key component of many minerals and is used in many industrial and construction applications.

81 Insects have been around for about 350 million years. They are one of the oldest groups of animals on Earth and have evolved to adapt to a wide variety of environments.

82 Porcupines are able to float on water due to the air spaces in their quills, which make them less dense than water.

83 Although it may seem like we can do multiple things at once, the brain is actually not capable of multitasking. Instead, it rapidly switches between tasks, giving the illusion of multitasking.

Largest organ in the human body

84 The skin is the largest organ in the human body, it has a total area of about 2 square meters. It serves as a barrier to protect the body from external elements, such as temperature changes and harmful substances, as well as helping to regulate body temperature and prevent water loss.

85 In Japan, it is possible to buy pyramid-shaped watermelons. These watermelons are grown in a pyramid-shaped mold, which gives them their unique shape.

86 A jar of Nutella is sold every 2.5 seconds. Nutella is a popular brand of chocolate and hazelnut spread, which is known for its smooth texture and delicious taste.

87 Sloths are known for their slow movements on land, but they are actually excellent swimmers and can hold their breath for up to 40 minutes while underwater.

88 The Goliath frog, found in Western Africa, is one of the largest frogs in the world, measuring up to 16 inches in length and weighing more than 7 pounds.

89 Bats are the only mammals that are capable of true flight. They are able to fly by using their wings, which are made up of a thin membrane of skin stretched over a network of bones.

90 Pandas are known to produce a lot of droppings, which can be recycled into paper. This is because pandas mostly eat bamboo, and bamboo is a fast-growing and sustainable source of pulp for paper-making.

91 The largest living organism on Earth is a fungus. The fungus Armillaria ostoyae is a type of honey mushroom and it covers over 2,200 acres of land in Oregon.

92 Hummingbirds are among the smallest birds in the world, with some species weighing less than a penny. They are able to hover in mid-air and fly backwards, making them highly maneuverable.

93 LEGO has an underground vault where they store every LEGO set ever produced.

94 The human heart beats approximately 115,000 times per day.

The Microbial World Inside Your Mouth

95 The human mouth is home to a diverse community of microorganisms, including bacteria, viruses, and fungi. While many of these microorganisms are harmless, some can cause oral health problems. An estimated billion bacteria can be found in the human mouth at any given time.

96 Most people fall asleep within seven minutes, however, this can vary depending on individual factors such as age, lifestyle, and health. Sleep is a complex process that is essential for physical and mental well-being, and disruptions to sleep can have serious consequences for health and quality of life.

97 Eyelashes have a growth cycle of about 150 days before they fall out. This can vary based on factors such as age, genetics, and overall health

98 The human body uses around 200 different muscles to walk, which work together to allow for movement and balance. The exact number can vary depending on the person and the specific actions involved.

99 Neutron stars are incredibly dense and compact objects, and they can rotate at incredibly high speeds, with some neutron stars spinning more than 600 times per second.

100 The Pyramid of Khufu, also known as the Great Pyramid, is the largest of the Egyptian pyramids located at Giza. It was built around 2580 BC as a tomb for the Egyptian pharaoh Khufu.

101 Theatre was invented by the ancient Greeks. They believed that theatre was a way to educate and entertain people while also honoring the gods. The ancient Greeks held festivals in honor of their gods, which included plays as part of the celebration.

102 New Zealand is an island country located in the southwestern Pacific Ocean. It is known for its large sheep population. Historically, sheep farming has been a major industry in New Zealand, and there are currently around 30 million sheep in the country, which is more than four times the human population.

103 "Rhythm" is the longest English word without a vowel, it has 7 letters in total.

The Curious Case of Venus

104 Venus has a very slow rotation, a day on Venus is longer than year, meaning that a day on Venus is about 243 Earth days and a year is about 225 Earth days.

105 The Great Wall of China is not visible from space with the naked eye. Despite popular belief, the Great Wall is not visible from low Earth orbit, as it is not wide enough to be seen from such a distance.

106 Ice cream, a sweet, creamy dessert, was once known as "cream ice." The name "ice cream" became more popular in the late 18th century. Ice cream is made by freezing a mixture of cream, sugar, and flavorings.

107 Sea otters often hold hands while they sleep to keep from drifting away from each other.

108 Mystery snails have the ability to regenerate their eyes completely after amputation through the mid-eyestalk. This is due to their ability to regenerate lost body parts.

109 The tallest mammal in the world is the giraffe, which can grow up to 18 feet tall. Giraffes are able to reach such great heights because of their long necks, which are made up of seven vertebrae that are elongated to allow them to reach leaves on tall trees.

110 The world's longest French fry is 34 inches long. This record was set in 2018 by a company in the United Kingdom.

111 Peanuts are not actually nuts. Peanuts are legumes, which means they are related to beans and lentils. They are grown underground and are known for their high protein content.

112 The Great Barrier Reef is the largest living structure on Earth. The Great Barrier Reef is a vast network of coral reefs that stretches for more than 1,400 miles along the coast of northeastern Australia. It is home to a wide variety of marine life and is visible from space.

Black hole

113 There is a supermassive black hole, with a mass of millions to billions of times the mass of the sun, located at the center of the Milky Way galaxy.

114 French fries, also known as chips or frites in some countries, are a popular side dish that originated in Belgium in the late 19th century. They are made by slicing potatoes into thin strips and then deep-frying them until they are crispy.

115 The Eiffel Tower was originally built as a temporary structure. It was built for the 1889 Paris Exposition and was meant to be taken down after 20 years. However, it was saved because it proved useful as a radio tower.

116 Tomatoes are a type of fruit that are often used as a vegetable in cooking. Botanically, tomatoes are classified as a fruit because they have seeds and develop from the ovary of a flower.

117 The United States has more television sets than the United Kingdom has people.

118 The first living creatures intentionally sent into space were fruit flies, which were used in experiments to study the effects of space travel on living organisms.

119 Olympus Mons on Mars is the tallest planetary mountain in the solar system, standing at a height of about 22 km or 72,000 ft.

120 Ham the Astrochimp was the first hominid to travel in space. He was launched into space on January 31, 1961, as part of the Mercury program.

121 In the past, Parents were able to send their children to their grandparents through postal services.

122 The number "four" is the only number with the same number of letters as its value.

123 Rubber bands can last longer when stored in a refrigerator.

The Humble Sponge

124 Sea sponges are considered to be the "least evolutionarily advanced" animal on the planet due to their simple body structure and lack of specialized organs or tissues.

125 When threatened, deer will sometimes flash the white underside of their tail as a warning signal to other deer in the area.

126 The longest river in the world is the Nile River. The Nile River is approximately 4,135 miles long, stretching through 11 countries in Africa, including Egypt, Sudan, and Ethiopia. It is the main water source for many of the people living along its banks, and it has played an important role in the history and development of the region.

127 The world's most poisonous animal is the box jellyfish, which has venom that can cause heart failure and death in just a few minutes.

128 A pizzly bear is a hybrid animal, the result of a polar bear mating with a grizzly bear. These hybrids are also known as grolar bears or nanulak. They are extremely rare, but have been observed in the wild in the Arctic regions of Canada and Alaska. Due to the decline of polar bear populations and the migration of grizzly bears into the Arctic, the likelihood of pizzly bears occurring in the wild may increase in the future.

129 The world's largest lizard is the Komodo dragon, which can grow up to 10 feet in length and weigh up to 150 pounds.

130 In 2006, a Coca-Cola employee named Joya Williams offered to sell trade secrets to Pepsi. Pepsi notified Coca-Cola, and the employee was later arrested and charged with theft. The incident highlights the importance of maintaining the confidentiality of trade secrets and the potential consequences of misusing them.

131 It is commonly believed that it would take a lot of time and technology to travel to space, however, in reality, it would only take an hour of driving to reach the edge of space.

Why are clouds white?

132 Clouds appear white because they are reflecting sunlight from above them. The light is scattered in all directions by the water droplets or ice crystals that make up the cloud, making it appear white to the human eye.

133 Crickets chirp at a rate that is related to the temperature of their environment. By counting the number of chirps a cricket makes in a second, and using a specific formula, you can estimate the temperature in degrees Fahrenheit.

134 On the popular children's television show Sesame Street, the character Cookie Monster is often shown eating cookies. In reality, these are actually rice cakes that are painted to resemble cookies.

135 Hummingbirds are able to fly in any direction, including backwards. They accomplish this by using their unique wing structure, which allows them to make quick, precise movements.

136 Pet hamsters have a lot of energy and can run up to 6 miles a night on a wheel. This is a good way to keep them physically active and healthy.

137 The world's largest reptile is the saltwater crocodile, which can grow up to 23 feet in length and weigh up to 2,200 pounds.

138 The world's fastest bird is the peregrine falcon, which can reach speeds of up to 240 mph when diving for prey.

139 The human eye is capable of detecting a wide range of colors, with estimates suggesting that it can detect around 10 million different colors. This is made possible by the presence of specialized cells called cones in the retina, which are sensitive to different wavelengths of light.

140 The world's largest mammal migration is the wildebeest migration in the Serengeti, in which over 1.5 million wildebeest, zebras, and gazelles travel over 1,800 miles in search of food and water.

The Mighty Cat Tail

141 Approximately 10% of a cat's total number of bones are found in its tail. This is because the tail is made up of a series of small bones called vertebrae, which allow the tail to move and express a wide range of emotions.

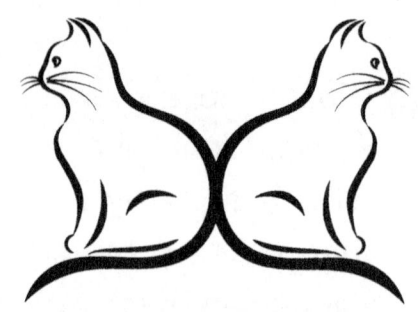

142 Human blood is a clear, red fluid that carries oxygen and nutrients to the body's cells and removes waste products. The salt concentration in human blood is similar to that of seawater, which helps to regulate the body's water balance and maintain the proper functioning of cells and organs.

143 Fingernails grow faster than toenails, about four times faster. This is because the blood flow to the fingers is greater than to the toes.

144 Easter Island, located in the Pacific Ocean, is home to 887 giant head statues known as Moai. These statues were carved by the island's inhabitants, the Rapa Nui people, nearly 2000 years ago. The purpose and method of transportation for the statues is still a mystery.

145 The Black Death, also known as the Bubonic Plague, was a devastating pandemic that swept through Europe in the 14th century. It is estimated that the disease killed nearly 75 million people, or roughly one third of the European population at the time.

146 The colossal squid has the largest eyes of any known animal, which can be as large as a soccer ball.

147 Anteaters, despite their name, do not have any teeth. Instead, they have long tongues and sharp claws to help them catch and eat ants and termites.

148 Viking men were known to wear makeup, particularly eyeliner, as it was believed to protect their eyes from the sun and enhance their appearance.

149 Eyeball tattooing is a form of body modification that involves injecting ink into the whites of the eyes. It is not a widely accepted practice and carries risks including blindness.

The Amazing Human Eye

150 The human eye is a complex organ made up of many different parts, including the cornea, iris, lens, retina, and optic nerve. It is estimated that the eye contains around 2 million working parts, but this number can vary depending on the source.

151 The nose and ears are made of cartilage, which does not stop growing when a person reaches maturity. As a result, these body parts may appear to grow larger over time.

152 Almonds are a type of nut that are actually a member of the rose family, Rosaceae, which also includes fruits such as peaches, plums, and apricots. The almond fruit is the seed of the almond tree, which is enclosed in a hard shell and surrounded by a fleshy outer layer.

153 Cranberries are a type of fruit that are often used in jams, jellies, and sauces. They are typically harvested when they are still hard and green, but when they are fully ripe, they can be bounced like a ball.

154 It is illegal to feed pigeons on the sidewalks and streets in San Francisco. This law was put in place to discourage the gathering of large numbers of pigeons in urban areas, as they can become a nuisance and pose a health risk. Violators may be subject to fines.

155 The Sulabh International Museum of Toilets in New Delhi, India, is a museum dedicated to the history of toilets and sanitation.

156 Three U.S. Presidents have won Grammy Awards: Jimmy Carter, Bill Clinton, and Barack Obama. The awards were given for their spoken word performances on audiobooks.

157 The Mpemba effect is a phenomenon in which hot water can freeze faster than cold water under certain conditions, such as when the water is in a container with a high surface area-to-volume ratio.

158 The average person farts about 14 times a day, and each fart travels out of the body at a speed of about 7 mph.

Australia's Rich History

159 Australia has a rich history of indigenous peoples, with evidence suggesting that these peoples have lived in the region for around 50,000 years before the arrival of the British.

160 The shortest complete sentence in the English language is "I Am."

161 Your fingernails may grow faster when your body is cold because the blood flow to the fingers and toes is decreased, which can lead to slower nail growth.

162 There are fossilized plants found in Greenland that are under 1.4 km of ice, indicating that the area has undergone significant changes in temperature and ice coverage over time.

163 The longest TV ad in history is 14 hours long, which is different from the typical 30-second to 1-minute commercials.

164 Pluto is considered a dwarf planet and is one of the five recognized by the International Astronomical Union, along with Ceres, Eris, Haumea, and Makemake.

165 Bears have an exceptional sense of smell, which is even better than that of dogs or any other mammal. This sense of smell is crucial for their survival as it helps them locate food and detect potential dangers.

166 Despite their white fur, polar bears have black skin. This is an adaptation to help them absorb more heat from the sun.

167 In Ancient Greece, it was common for athletes to exercise and compete in the nude. This was considered to be a sign of physical beauty and strength. The Greeks had a strong emphasis on the importance of physical fitness and the human body, and nudity in athletic competitions was an accepted practice.

168 The average life expectancy in Ancient Rome was between 20 and 30 years due to various factors such as lack of proper sanitation, poor nutrition, and a high incidence of disease.

Farthest human-made object from Earth

169 Spacecraft such as Voyager 1 and Voyager 2 have been traveling through the solar system for decades . oyager 1 is currently the farthest human-made object from Earth, having crossed the heliopause, the boundary where the solar wind meets the interstellar medium.

170 Over the past 500 years, human actions such as habitat destruction, hunting, and introduction of non-native species have led to the extinction of 322 animal species.

171 The conflicts between the Roman and Persian empires lasted for approximately 721 years. This long-term conflict had a Crucial impact on both empires and their neighboring regions.

172 Some small animals have been observed to perceive time at a slower rate than humans. This is due to their faster neural processing speed and different neural encoding. This allows them to process more information in a shorter amount of time, which can give them an advantage in certain situations, such as hunting.

173 The wood frog, along with other species of animals, has the ability to survive freezing temperatures by entering a state of suspended animation known as cryopreservation. This allows them to survive the harsh winter conditions.

174 African elephants are known to have the most developed sense of smell among all animals, which they use for finding food and for detecting potential dangers.

175 Hiroshima and Nagasaki were the two cities that were destroyed by atomic bombings at the end of World War II. While the bombings resulted in radiation contamination, decontamination efforts have been undertaken in the years since, and the cities are not considered radioactive today.

176 The circulatory system, which includes the heart and blood vessels, is over 60,000 miles in length.

177 Birds have the ability to fly, but they cannot survive in space because they rely on gravity to swallow food.

The Sound of Silence

178 The quietest place on Earth, an anechoic chamber, can reach sound levels as low as -9 decibels. The human ear can perceive sounds as low as 0 decibels, and prolonged exposure to extremely low levels of noise can be uncomfortable for some people.

179 Humans are the only primates with a distinct protrusion of the jawbone, known as a chin. Some scientists believe that the chin may have evolved as a way to support the jaw muscles and improve the efficiency of chewing.

180 Spain, Sweden and Switzerland remained neutral in World War II and did not join any side. They did not participate in the war, but they were still affected by it.

181 George Washington, the first President of the United States, opened a whiskey distillery after his presidential term. Washington was a successful farmer and businessman, and the distillery was part of his Mount Vernon estate. He used the profits from the distillery to fund his retirement.

182 The ancient Romans used urine as a cleaning agent, and some sources suggest that they also used it as a mouthwash. Urine was collected from public toilets and was believed to have antiseptic properties.

183 India was the only known source of diamonds until the discovery of diamonds in South Africa in 1896. This made India the world's leading diamond producer for centuries.

184 The Mayan civilization, which existed in Mesoamerica from about 2000 BC to 900 AD, had a complex religious system. The turkey was revered and considered sacred by the Mayans and played a role in their religious ceremonies.

185 While you sleep, your sense of smell is temporarily impaired, This is because the olfactory bulbs are active during wakefulness but become less active during sleep.

186 An astronaut named Edgar Mitchell, who was part of the Apollo 14 mission in 1971, claimed to have developed an allergic reaction to the moon dust. However, this has not been confirmed by any scientific evidence.

Closest Planet to the Sun

187 Mercury is the closest planet to the Sun and has a much shorter orbital period than Earth, taking approximately 88 Earth days to orbit the Sun.

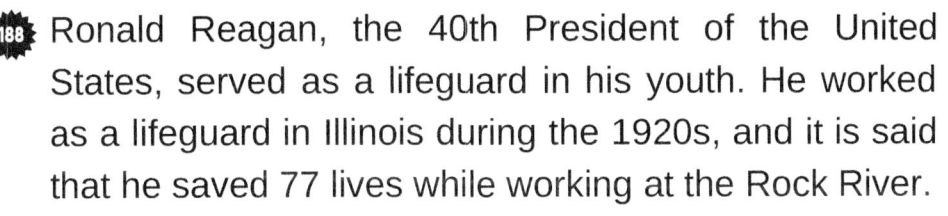

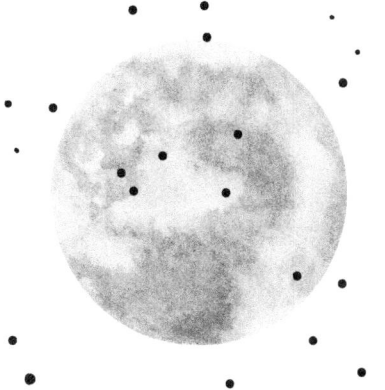

188 Ronald Reagan, the 40th President of the United States, served as a lifeguard in his youth. He worked as a lifeguard in Illinois during the 1920s, and it is said that he saved 77 lives while working at the Rock River.

189 Steve Jobs, the co-founder of Apple, was known for his attention to design and this extended to his deathbed. He requested five different oxygen masks to choose from.

190 Alaska, the largest state in the United States by area, was formerly a part of the Russian Empire until its purchase by the United States in 1867. The acquisition cost $7.2 million, which is equivalent to $12.5 per square mile of land.

191 The name "Amazon" is believed to come from the Greek mythology's "Amazons", a race of woman warriors. The name was given to the river and the region by the Spanish explorer Francisco de Orellana in 1541, who named it after encountering indigenous women who reminded him of the Amazons in Greek legends.

192 The bumblebee bat, also known as the Kitti's hog-nosed bat, is the smallest mammal in the world, with a wingspan of only about 6 centimeters.

193 Snails are known for their slow movements, but they also have long periods of rest, called estivation. During estivation, a snail can remain inactive for up to three years.

194 Bees can sting other bees when they feel threatened or are protecting their territory, similar to how humans may react when feeling threatened or defending their space.

195 Christianity, Islam, Hinduism, Chinese folk religion, and Buddhism are the five most widely practiced religions in the world. All these religions have their origins in different parts of Asia and have played a Vital role in shaping the culture and society of the region.

World's Biggest Oxygen Producers

196 Approximately 50% of the Earth's oxygen is produced by phytoplankton and other photosynthetic organisms in the ocean. These organisms use energy from the sun to convert carbon dioxide and water into oxygen and sugar, a process known as photosynthesis.

197 Water can exist in a state known as "supercooled," in which it remains liquid below its freezing point. Under certain conditions, supercooled water can freeze instantly when it comes into contact with a solid surface, a process known as "flash freezing.

198 Crocodiles are unable to stick their tongues out as their tongues are attached to the bottom of their mouths.

199 The name "Pluto" for the dwarf planet was proposed by an 11-year-old girl named Venetia Burney, who was inspired by the Roman god of the underworld.

200 China has reportedly cloned a police dog that had previously won awards for its service. This is done by using the same genetic material from the original dog to create a new, identical animal.

201 Indonesia is known to have some of the shortest people in the world. The average height of the Indonesian population is relatively low compared to other countries.

202 Infants are born with around 300 bones, while adults have 206 bones. This is because some bones fuse together as a child grows and develops.

203 Cats, domestic animals, have been known to manipulate their owners by making vocalizations that sound similar to that of a crying baby.

204 Leo Tolstoy, a Russian novelist, took six years to complete his famous novel "War and Peace."

205 Anne Jones, the world speed-reading champion, holds the record for reading all 607 pages of the last Harry Potter book in just 47 minutes.

Eiffel Tower's Summer Growth

206 The Eiffel Tower can appear to grow taller during the summer months because of thermal expansion. As the temperature increases, the metal of the tower expands, causing it to increase in length by as much as 6 inches.

207 Ninety-Mile Beach, located in New Zealand, is actually not 90 miles long. Instead, it is around 55 miles long. The beach got its name due to a miscommunication between early settlers and the indigenous Maori people.

208 Chicken today contains 266% more fat than it did 40 years ago. This increase in fat content is due to changes in the way chickens are raised and fed.

209 In 2008, Norway knighted a penguin named Nils Olav at Edinburgh Zoo in Scotland. Nils Olav is a king penguin and was given the rank of "Brigadier" in the Norwegian King's Guard.

210 All pandas in the world are on loan from China. This is because all pandas in the world belong to China and are loaned out to other countries through a process called "panda diplomacy." As part of this process, countries that wish to host pandas must agree to certain terms and conditions, including breeding and conservation efforts.

211 There is a skyscraper in New York City called "The New York Times Building" that does not have any windows on its exterior walls. The building was designed this way to reduce energy consumption and improve energy efficiency.

212 All prisoners in Norway have access to the internet in their cells. This policy is part of Norway's focus on rehabilitation and reintegration into society, rather than punishment.

213 Dolphin meat is consumed in some countries, such as Japan and Peru. However, this practice is controversial due to the fact that dolphins are highly intelligent and social animals, and many conservationists and animal welfare activists consider it to be inhumane.

214 The brand name "Spam" is a combination of the words "spice" and "ham", reflecting the product's main ingredients.

215 The moon is gradually moving away from the Earth at a rate of approximately 3.78 centimeters per year. This is due to a process known as lunar recession, which is caused by the gravitational pull of the Earth on the moon.

216 There is a large amount of gold inside Earth. The total amount of gold that has been mined throughout history is estimated to be around 170,000 tons, which is only a tiny fraction of the total amount of gold present in the Earth's crust.

217 The average depth of the ocean is about 2.5 miles (4 km). Although the ocean is a vast and diverse environment, the majority of it is relatively shallow. However, there are also some deep trenches and canyons that reach depths of several miles, making them some of the most extreme environments on Earth.

218 The origins of high heels can be traced back to men, specifically Persian soldiers, who wore them to help grip their stirrups while riding horses. However, over time, high heels became associated with women's fashion.

219 San Francisco was not always a part of the United States. Prior to the Mexican-American War in the 1840s, the area now known as San Francisco was part of Mexico.

220 The name "Jesus" in Hebrew is Yeshua, which is translated to Joshua in English. The name Jesus is derived from the Greek form of the name Iesous, which is then translated to Latin and English.

221 Honey is a food that has antimicrobial properties which allows it to last longer than many other foods and does not spoil easily but it can crystallize over time.

222 Penguins have a limited sense of taste and can only taste sour and salty flavors. They are not able to taste sweet flavors.

223 Pandas can defecate up to 40 times per day. This is due to their diet, which consists mostly of bamboo, which is low in nutrients and high in fiber.

224 In the movie "Fight Club", a Starbucks coffee cup can be seen in almost every single scene.

225 The world's first novel, "The Tale of Genji" by Murasaki Shikibu, ends abruptly in the middle of a sentence, as it is believed that the author did not live to finish it.

226 The boiling point of water decreases as altitude increases. At the summit of Mount Everest, which stands at 29,029 feet above sea level, the boiling point of water is approximately 71 degrees Celsius (159.8 degrees Fahrenheit) due to the lower atmospheric pressure.

227 In the past, sea levels were much different than they are today. This is due to changes in the Earth's climate, as well as the movement of tectonic plates and the growth or melting of ice sheets.

228 Coca-Cola, is a popular brand, with products sold in more than 200 countries and territories.

229 Phobophobia is the fear of having a phobia. It is a type of anxiety disorder that can cause people to fear the development of a phobia or the symptoms of a phobia.

230 The average person unlocks their smartphone 110 times per day. This frequent use of mobile devices has become a common aspect of modern life, but it can also lead to overuse and addiction.

231 The world's largest man-made oyster reef is located in Chesapeake Bay, Maryland. It was created to help restore the oyster population and improve water quality in the bay.

232 Butterflies have taste receptors on their feet, which they use to detect chemicals in their food.

233 New York City is known for its wealth, and according to a survey by Spectrem Group, 1 out of every 21 residents of the city is a millionaire.

234 Octopuses are known for their ability to change color, and the skin of an octopus can change color up to 177 times in one hour. This camouflage is used to blend in with their surroundings and to communicate with other octopuses.

235 Australia was once referred to as "New Holland" by early European explorers, and it wasn't until the early 19th century that it began to be known by its current name.

236 In the United States, the consumption of animals for food is very high, with an estimated 9 billion chickens and 150 million cattle, pigs, and sheep being consumed annually.

237 Antarctica is the coldest continent on Earth, with temperatures reaching as low as -128.6 °F (-89.2 °C). The highest temperature ever recorded on the continent was 58.2°F (14.5°C).

238 Mary, Queen of Scots, was crowned as the Queen of Scotland at the age of six days old, following the death of her father, King James V.

239 Sour Patch Kids and Swedish Fish are made by the same manufacturer, and the red Sour Patch Kids are the same candy as Swedish Fish, but coated in sour sugar.

240 Wild tigers are an important symbol of Asia's biodiversity, but their numbers have drastically declined over the past century. A century ago, there were an estimated 100,000 wild tigers in Asia, but today, due to poaching and habitat loss, their numbers have fallen to around 3,200.

Can Bears See In Color?

241 Many mammals have poor color vision, but bears are an exception. They have the ability to see in color, which is an adaptation that helps them locate food and navigate their environment.

242 Charlie Chaplin was honored with an honorary Academy Award in 1972, and when he received it, he was greeted with a 12-minute standing ovation – the longest in Oscar history.

243 Alexander the Great was a military leader who, during a 15-year period of conquest, never lost a battle. He was able to conquer a vast empire that stretched from Greece all the way to India. His military tactics and leadership skills were considered to be exceptional, which contributed to his string of victories.

244 The Retina display used in the Apple iPad is actually manufactured by Samsung, a South Korean electronics company.

245 Pato, a traditional sport that combines elements of polo and basketball played on horseback, is considered the national sport of Argentina, not soccer.

246 In Lionel Messi's hometown in Argentina, government officials have banned parents from naming their children "Messi."

247 The vast majority of bananas consumed worldwide belong to the species Musa acuminata and Musa balbisiana.

248 Strawberries are not classified as a true berry botanically speaking, because the fleshy part of the fruit is not derived from the ovary, but bananas are botanically classified as a berry because the fleshy part of the fruit develops from the ovary.

249 Kangaroos, marsupials native to Australia, are unable to move backwards due to the structure of their hind legs and tail.

250 While shark attacks are a concern for swimmers and surfers, the number of deaths caused by taking selfies in 2015 was actually higher. According to a study by the All India Institute of Medical Sciences, more than half of all selfie-related deaths that year were caused by drowning.

251 A large portion of all gold ever mined on Earth is estimated to have come from a single plateau in South Africa, called Witwatersrand. This area has been a major source of gold mining for over a century.

252 Approximately 40-80% of the population in Classical Athens were slaves, they were considered property and did not have any legal rights. They were used for a variety of tasks such as agriculture, mining, and household work.

253 Alexander the Great had a condition known as heterochromia iridum, where one of his eyes was blue and the other was brown. This is a rare genetic condition that affects the pigmentation of the eyes.

254 At present, humans are killing a large number of animals for food, with a rate of approximately 1,776 animals per second. This high rate of animal consumption is contributing to the loss of biodiversity and deforestation.

255 In the United States, it is illegal to collect eagle feathers without proper authorization, as eagles and their feathers are protected under federal law. Violators can face fines and even jail time.

256 In Japan, Kit Kat candy bars were released in sushi-inspired flavors, such as "Tuna Mayo" and "Salmon Roe."

257 Cows, like many other four-legged animals, are able to walk up stairs but have difficulty walking down them because of the way their joints are structured.

258 During the Stone Age, the entire population of Central Europe could have fit on a single cruise ship, indicating that the population was relatively small at that time.

259 "Stewardesses" is considered to be the longest word that can be typed using only the left hand on a standard keyboard.

Why Apple ads always display 9:41 AM?

260 Apple iPhone ads typically display the time as 9:41 AM, which is the time that the original iPhone was announced on January 9, 2007, at the Macworld conference.

261 The Mona Lisa, a famous painting by Leonardo da Vinci, is known for her enigmatic smile, but many people may not know that the painting is also missing eyebrows.

262 Sudan has more pyramids than any other country in the world, due to its rich history and ancient civilization.

263 Usain Bolt, the famous Jamaican sprinter, owns a 3-ton segment of the Berlin Wall. He purchased it at an auction in 2011 as a symbol of his success and the power of overcoming obstacles.

264 Leonardo da Vinci, a famous artist and inventor of the Renaissance period, was known to purchase caged animals for the purpose of studying their anatomy and behavior.

265 The tongue is a muscle that is responsible for many functions such as speaking, tasting and swallowing. It is also considered one of the strongest muscles in the body, as it is able to move food around in the mouth and manipulate it before swallowing.

266 At birth, babies do not have bacteria in their bodies. However, they will quickly acquire it from their environment through means such as the mother's birth canal, breastmilk, and surrounding surfaces.

267 The brain is the heaviest organ in the human body, weighing on average about 3 pounds.

268 Newborn babies have a small amount of blood in their bodies, approximately 80-100 milliliters, which is roughly equivalent to one cup.

269 Research has suggested that individuals with autism may be less likely to experience contagious yawning, which is the tendency to yawn when someone else yawns.

270 For 16 years, tomato ketchup was used as a medicine for various ailments.

271 Jellyfish are known to be some of the most efficient swimmers in the ocean. They are able to move through the water with minimal effort and can cover great distances with ease. This makes them unique among marine animals and scientists are still trying to understand the mechanisms that allow them to swim so efficiently.

272 The Holocaust was a systematic extermination of Jews and other minority groups during World War II, and a large number of people were killed in concentration camps, including Auschwitz. The number of Jewish deaths in the Holocaust is estimated to be around six million, and it is estimated that about one in six of those deaths occurred at Auschwitz.

273 In Arizona, cutting down a cactus is considered a serious offense and can result in a penalty of up to 25 years in jail, similar to the penalties for cutting down a protected tree species.

274 Hawaii is considered to be one of the best places in the world to see rainbows.

275 According to Japanese legend, it is believed that if one folds 1,000 origami cranes, they will be granted a wish by the gods.

Traveling around the Sun

276 It would take significantly longer to travel around the Sun than it would to orbit Earth, as the distance from the Sun to Earth is much shorter than the distance needed to travel around the Sun.

277 In 2013, there were reports of jellyfish clogging the cooling systems of nuclear power plants, which could have potentially caused mass nuclear explosions. However, it is important to note that these incidents were not as widespread or severe as implied, and the power plants have measures in place to prevent such occurrences.

278 There has been an increase in the number of twins born in recent years, this is due to the availability and use of fertility treatments, as well as an increase in the number of older mothers.

279 Alarm clocks have been used for centuries to wake people up at a specific time. However, before alarm clocks were invented, people used alarm humans, which were individuals who were hired to wake people up at a specific time.

280 The oldest webcam stream online is The San Francisco FogCam, which has been in operation since 1994. This webcam is located on the roof of San Francisco State University and streams live footage of the city's famous fog. The FogCam is considered one of the first webcams in the world and has been running continuously since its creation, making it a unique historical artifact of the early days of the internet.

281 Cans of diet soda are less dense than cans of regular soda, which means they will float in water. Regular soda cans, on the other hand, are denser, and will sink in water.

282 Pigs are unable to look up into the sky due to the structure of their necks and the position of their eyes.

283 Three US Presidents have won Grammy Awards: Jimmy Carter, Bill Clinton and Barack Obama.

284 An octopus is a highly adaptable animal and will do whatever it takes to survive. In extreme cases of hunger, an octopus may resort to eating its own arms in order to stay alive.

285 Papaphobia is a fear of the Pope. People with this phobia may experience anxiety, panic attacks or other symptoms when they are in the presence of the Pope or when they think about him. This phobia is relatively rare but can be severe and debilitating for those who suffer from it.

286 Peaches and nectarines are nearly identical genetically, with the main difference being the presence of a fuzzy skin on peaches.

287 The origin of Hawaiian pizza is often attributed to Canada, where it was first created in 1962.

288 Hippopotamuses are not as slow as one might think, they can run at a speed of up to 20 miles per hour. This is faster than the average human running speed.

289 The heart of a prawn is located at the base of its head. This location allows the prawn to pump blood to the rest of its body, including its gills, where the blood is oxygenated.

290 Bees are found in nearly every part of the world, with the exception of Antarctica. They are important pollinators and play a vital role in many ecosystems.

291 Some theories suggest that black holes may be able to give birth to new universes through a process known as "quantum tunneling."

292 The largest living organism on Earth is the giant sequoia tree, which can reach up to 379 feet in height and 26 feet in diameter.

293. The blue color of the ocean is caused by the scattering of sunlight by the water. When sunlight hits the ocean, water molecules scatter the light in all directions. Blue light has a shorter wavelength than other colors and is scattered more easily, making the ocean appear blue.

294. YouTube's "subscribe" button was not added until 2011, five years after the site's launch. This feature allows users to subscribe to a channel and receive updates when new videos are uploaded, and it has become an important way for creators to build and engage with their audience.

295. Black holes also emit radiation called Hawking radiation, which causes them to slowly lose mass over time, a process known as evaporation.

296. Antarctica is the only continent on Earth without any reptiles or snakes. This is because the harsh and cold climate of Antarctica is not conducive to the survival and reproduction of reptiles and snakes, which are cold-blooded animals that require warmer temperatures to survive. Additionally, the lack of native mammals and other food sources in Antarctica also makes it an unsuitable habitat for these animals.

297. Daniel Radcliffe, the actor who played Harry Potter in the film series, has said that he had an allergic reaction to the glasses he wore in the movies. He explained that the paint used on the frames caused an allergic rash on the skin around his eyes. The production team had to rewrite certain scenes in order to conceal the rash and avoid filming close-ups of his face.

298. It is possible to get your eyeballs tattooed, but it is not recommended as it can lead to severe eye infections, blindness, and even permanent damage to your vision.

299. Grapes can light on fire in the microwave because of their unique composition. Grapes contain small amounts of water and natural sugar. When microwaved, the grapes heat up and cause a spark which can ignite the sugar.

300. The brain uses 10 watts of energy to function and does not have the ability to feel pain.

301 The small intestine, despite its name, is actually the largest internal organ in the human body. Its primary function is to absorb nutrients from food.

302 Ancient Egyptians had a complex pantheon of more than 2,000 deities whom they worshipped in various forms of religious rituals and ceremonies. They believed that these gods and goddesses controlled the forces of nature and governed human fate.

303 Stonehenge, located in Wiltshire, England, is a prehistoric monument that is believed to have been built over a period of nearly 1500 years, beginning around 3000 BC. The purpose of the monument is still debated, but it is believed to have been used for religious or ceremonial purposes.

304 The oldest known living organism is a bristlecone pine tree in California, which is estimated to be over 5,000 years old.

305 The world's largest volcano is Mauna Loa on the island of Hawaii, which rises up to 30,080 feet above sea level and has a volume of about 18,000 cubic miles.

306 The world's tallest animal is the giraffe, which can grow up to 18 feet in height.

307 The world's fastest land animal is the cheetah, which can reach speeds of up to 75 mph.

308 The world's largest bird is the ostrich, which can weigh up to 345 pounds and stand up to 9 feet tall.

309 Michael Phelps, a renowned Olympic swimmer, struggled with mental health issues after the 2012 Summer Olympics, and even considered suicide. He later started the Michael Phelps Foundation to help others with similar struggles.

310 It has been over 50 years since a plane crash was caused by lighting. The last recorded incident was in 1963.

311 Consuming six or more cups of coffee per day has been linked to an increased risk of heart disease, by up to 22%.

312. The heart can change its size and shape depending on the body's needs. The heart can shrink or expand to adjust the amount of blood it pumps and the rate at which it pumps it. This is known as cardiac remodeling.

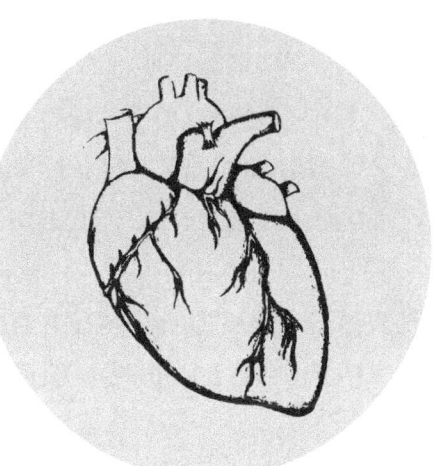

313. Salamanders are capable of regenerating lost body parts, including tails, legs, and even parts of their eyes.

314. Earthworms are hermaphrodites, meaning they possess both male and female reproductive organs and can self-fertilize.

315. Chameleons have extremely long tongues, often measuring up to twice the length of their body, which they use to capture their prey.

316. Slugs have two pairs of sensory tentacles on their head, which are often referred to as "noses." These tentacles are used to sense their surroundings and locate food.

317. The world's longest concert lasted 453 hours and was performed by the band "The Flaming Lips" in Oklahoma City, USA in 2012. The concert lasted 18 days and 17 hours.

318. Four out of the ten largest statues in the world are of Buddhas. These statues include the Spring Temple Buddha in China, the Ushiku Daibutsu in Japan, the Laykyun Sekkya in Myanmar, and the Tian Tan Buddha in Hong Kong.

319. Each dog has a unique nose print, similar to how human fingerprints are unique.

320. This can be used as a form of identification for dogs.

321. Male toads are known to make croaking sounds, while females do not. This is likely used as a means of communication between males during breeding season.

322. Dogs have a highly developed sense of smell, with the ability to detect odors at a concentration 100,000 times lower than that of humans.

Largest river in the world by discharge

323 The Amazon River, which runs through the rainforest, is the largest river in the world by discharge and the second longest by length. There are no bridges over the Amazon River, making it difficult to cross without a boat or ferry.

324 It is also believed that The Amazon River once flowed in the opposite direction, from east to west, due to the ancient tectonic plate movements.

325 The Amazon Rainforest is known for its diverse array of species, including approximately 2.5 million insect species. One such insect found in the region is the butterfly, which is known to drink the tears of turtles for their salt content.

326 Humans and chimpanzees share a close genetic relationship, with 99% of their DNA being identical.

327 The world's oldest wooden wheel is more than 5,000 years old. It was discovered in the ruins of an ancient settlement in Slovenia and is believed to have been used for transportation purposes. The wheel is made of ash and oak wood and is considered to be an important artifact of ancient civilizations.

328 Moonquakes are seismic events that occur on the surface of the Moon. They are less common than earthquakes on Earth because the Moon has a much smaller and less active core, and its crust is not being actively deformed by plate tectonics.

329 An astronaut named Edgar Mitchell experienced an allergic reaction to moon dust during the Apollo 14 mission in 1971.

330 There is a toilet museum in New Delhi, India called Sulabh International Museum of Toilets.

331 The human body is home to trillions of bacteria, and their collective weight is estimated to be around 4 pounds.

332 Amazon's largest warehouse is massive, covering an area equivalent to 17 American football fields.

333 Consuming large amounts of carrots can lead to a condition called carotenemia, which causes the skin to turn orange due to excessive levels of beta-carotene in the body.

334 The Canary Islands are named after the Latin word "canaria," which means "dog," likely in reference to the island's wild dogs that were present when the Romans first visited. The name has nothing to do with birds, although the islands are home to many different species of birds.

335 The state of Rhode Island could fit into the state of Alaska 425 times based on their respective land areas.

336 Research suggests that an actor's brain activity may change when they are in character, as they may be utilizing different neural pathways to embody the role.

337 Coca-Cola is not widely available in North Korea and Cuba due to economic and political reasons.

338 Goats have a unique shape to their pupils, which are rectangular in shape. This is thought to help them with peripheral vision and spotting predators.

339 Studies have found that women blink more often than men, potentially due to differences in hormones or societal expectations of appearance.

340 Vatican City is the smallest sovereign state in the world, measuring approximately 0.2 square miles in area.

341 The Philippines is made up of a large number of islands, with an estimated total of 7,641.

342 Abraham Lincoln, the 16th President of the United States, was known for his tall stature at 6'4. He was also a successful wrestler in his youth, winning several matches.

343 X-ray machines were once used in shoe shops to measure the length and width of astomer's foot, which helped to determine their shoe size.

344 The attack on the World Trade Center on September 11, 2001 resulted in the deadliest terrorist attack in world history and the single deadliest incident for firefighters and law enforcement officers in the history of the United States, with 2,977 deaths.

345 The state flag of Alaska was designed by a 13-year-old boy named Benny Benson in the 1920s as part of a contest for young children.

346 The Amazon rainforest, located primarily in Brazil and spanning across nine other countries, is the largest rainforest in the world, covering an area of over 5.5 million square kilometers. It is known for its biodiversity, with an estimated 400 billion individual trees belonging to over 16,000 species.

347 It is believed that human inhabitants first settled in the Amazon rainforest at least 11,200 years ago. The forest has been in existence for at least 55 million years, and has been a vital part of the Earth's ecosystem for that entire time.

348 The Amazon rainforest is also known for its high levels of biodiversity, with an estimated 1 in 10 known species in the world living there. This includes a wide variety of plants and animals, many of which are not found anywhere else in the world.

349 Working in Antarctica comes with certain medical requirements, including the removal of wisdom teeth and the appendix.

350 Antarctica is the only continent without a time zone and has over 300 subglacial lakes that are kept from freezing by the warmth of the Earth's core.

351 Asia is a major producer and consumer of rice, with an estimated 90% of all rice produced in the world consumed within the region.

352 The population of kangaroos in Australia is higher than that of human residents.

353 The first ozone hole was discovered over Antarctica in 1985, and it is still healing, but at a slow pace due to the long lifespan of ozone-depleting chemicals.

The first known democracy in the world

354 The first known democracy in the world was established in Ancient Greece, specifically in Athens. This system of government, where citizens had a direct say in the laws and policies of the state, lasted for 185 years. Although it only applied to a small portion of the population, it was a Valuable development.

355 Alexander the Great was tutored by the philosopher Aristotle until the age of 16. Aristotle was a renowned thinker and teacher of his time, and his teachings on politics, ethics, and logic had a Crucial impact on Alexander's education and worldview.

356 In Ancient Rome, urine was sometimes used as a cleaning agent for laundry. Urine contains ammonia which was used as a cleaning agent. But it was not a common practice and only done by the poor people.

357 During the time the Berlin Wall existed, around 5,000 individuals attempted to escape from East Germany to West Germany by crossing the wall. Many of these attempts were successful, but some resulted in injury or death.

358 A large portion of animal populations in tropical rainforests, as much as 70%, rely on figs as a primary source of food for their survival.

359 In 2001, there was a political crisis in Argentina that resulted in five different presidents serving within a 10-day period.

360 The human heart can respond to music by syncing its rhythm with the beat of the music.

361 The human heart can also beat outside the body, but this typically only occurs in the context of medical procedures such as heart transplantation.

362 The first video ever uploaded to YouTube was entitled "Me at the zoo" and was uploaded by a user named Jawed Karim. The video, which was uploaded on April 23, 2005, is just over 18 seconds long and features Karim talking about elephants at the San Diego Zoo.

363. The world's largest mammal is the blue whale, which can weigh up to 200 tons and reach lengths of up to 100 feet.

364. The world's smallest mammal is the bumblebee bat, which weighs less than a penny and is about the size of a thumb.

365. The average temperature on Mars is much colder than the Earth's South Pole, with temperatures dropping as low as -125°C.

366. The world's largest fish is the whale shark, which can grow up to 40 feet in length and weigh up to 20 tons.

367. The world's largest insect is the goliath beetle, which can grow up to 4 inches in length and weigh up to 4 ounces.

368. The world's most venomous snake is the Inland Taipan, also known as the Fierce Snake, which has venom that can kill a human in less than an hour.

369. The world's largest amphibian is the Chinese giant salamander, which can grow up to 6 feet in length.

370. The world's largest reptile is the saltwater crocodile, which can grow up to 23 feet in length and weigh up to 2,200 pounds.

371. The world's fastest bird is the peregrine falcon, which can reach speeds of up to 240 mph when diving for prey.

372. The world's largest crab is the Japanese spider crab, which can have a leg span of up to 12 feet and weigh up to 42 pounds.

373. The world's largest mammal migration is the Journey of Humpback whales, in which over 20,000 Humpback whales travel annually from the polar waters to tropical breeding grounds.

374. The world's highest waterfall is Angel Falls in Venezuela, which drops a total of 3,212 feet.

375 The world's largest waterfall by volume is the Iguazu Falls in South America, which has an average flow rate of 62,010 cubic feet per second.

376 The world's largest desert is the Antarctic Desert, which covers about 5.5 million square miles.

377 Saturn's rings are primarily composed of ice particles, including water ice, and dust

378 YouTube was originally created as a dating site, with the idea that users could upload videos of themselves to attract potential partners. This was the original concept behind the website, but it quickly evolved into a platform for sharing all types of videos.

379 The heart has its own electrical system that controls the heartbeat. The sinoatrial (SA) node and atrioventricular (AV) node are two specialized areas within the heart that generate electrical impulses to coordinate the contraction of the heart's chambers.

380 The heart can repair itself. After a heart attack, the heart can form new blood vessels and muscle cells to repair the damage. However, the extent of recovery depends on the severity of the damage.

381 Flight Sergeant Nicholas Alkemade was a British airman who survived a fall from 18,000 feet (5,486 meters) without a parachute during World War II.

382 Oscars, faced a shortage of metals and other materials due to the war effort. As a result, in 1943, the Oscar statuettes were made of painted plaster instead of the typical metal (which was made of Britannia metal, an alloy of tin, antimony, and copper), and this continued until the end of the war in 1945.

Human Body

383 The human body has a natural defense mechanism known as the "innate immune system" which can recognize and respond to pathogens without prior exposure. This includes physical and chemical barriers, such as the skin and mucus, as well as cellular responses, such as inflammation and fever.

384 The human nose is capable of recognizing and distinguishing between a vast array of different scents. It is estimated that the human nose can distinguish between 50,000 different scents, thanks to the olfactory receptors located in the nasal cavity. These receptors can detect and respond to different chemicals in the air, allowing us to perceive different smells.

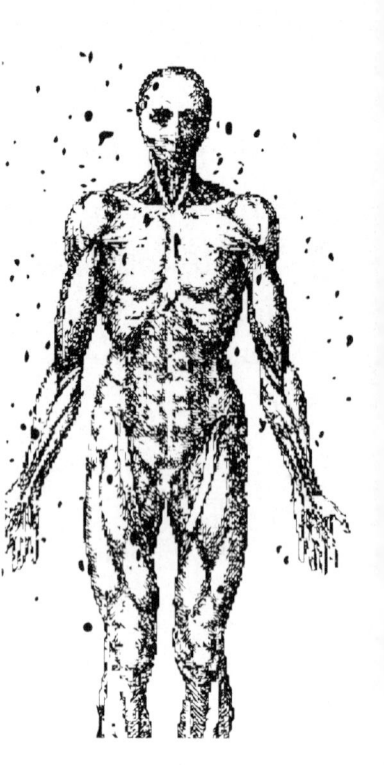

385 The human body contains a significant amount of iron, which is an essential mineral required for various bodily functions. Iron is present in red blood cells, which carry oxygen throughout the body, and in muscles, where it helps in the formation of hemoglobin. The total amount of iron in an adult human body is estimated to be around 3 to 4 grams. This amount of iron is enough to make a small nail of about 3 inches long.

386 During World War II, many members of the Muslim community in France, including the Grand Mosque of Paris, did help Jews escape persecution by the Nazis by providing them with false Muslim identities and papers.

387 The World War I ended on November 11, 1918, with the signing of the Armistice of Compiègne between the Allies and Germany. The armistice was signed at 5:00 a.m. and it came into effect at 11:00 a.m. (Paris time), on the 11th day of the 11th month of 1918, which is why it is traditionally referred to as the "11th hour of the 11th day of the 11th month."

388 The prevalence of autism diagnosis is higher in boys compared to girls, with 1 out of 42 boys and 1 in 189 girls being diagnosed with autism.

389. The lion is widely recognized as the second-largest living cat species, after the tiger. Lions are known for their majestic appearance and powerful roar, and they play a key role in many of the world's ecosystems.

390. "Big Ben" is a popular nickname for the Great Bell of the clock at the north end of the Palace of Westminster in London, but it is not the tower itself. The nickname has since been applied to the entire tower, which is now officially known as the Elizabeth Tower.

391. While physical beauty is subjective and can play a role in attracting romantic partners, studies have shown that a beautiful face tends to be a more important factor than a beautiful body. People often place a higher value on facial symmetry and facial features when assessing physical attractiveness.

392. The famous lion that appears at the start of MGM movies is named "Leo the Lion." This regal mascot has become an iconic symbol of the studio and is widely recognized as one of the most famous movie logos in the world.

393. The issue of marijuana use and its regulation is a complex and controversial one in the United States. According to some estimates, over 800,000 people are arrested each year for marijuana-related offenses, but this number can vary depending on local laws and enforcement practices.

394. Abraham Lincoln was the 16th President of the United States and served in this role from 1861 until his assassination in 1865. He is widely regarded as one of America's greatest Presidents and is remembered for his leadership during the Civil War, as well as for his efforts to abolish slavery and preserve the Union.

395. In the 1950s, Las Vegas was a city on the rise and was quickly becoming known for its thriving entertainment industry. During this time, a Miss Atomic Bomb beauty contest was held, which was designed to promote the city's ties to the nuclear weapons testing that was taking place nearby. The winner of the contest was crowned "Miss Atomic Bomb" and became a symbol of the city's connection to the nuclear industry.

396. Ants typically take around 8 minutes of rest within a 12-hour period.

397 Islam is the world's second-largest religion, with over 1.8 billion followers worldwide. It is also the fastest-growing religion, with an estimated conversion rate of nearly 2 million people per year. Islam is based on the teachings of the prophet Muhammad and is practiced primarily in the Middle East, North Africa, and Southeast Asia.

398 Over 5,000 climbers have successfully reached the summit of Mount Everest, the highest peak in the world. However, climbing the mountain is extremely dangerous, and many people have lost their lives attempting the climb.

399 Nomophobia is a term used to describe the fear of being without a mobile phone or losing your signal. This fear can manifest as anxiety, stress, and even panic attacks, and it is becoming increasingly common in today's highly connected world.

400 In Siberia, prior to World War II, tea bricks were used as a form of currency. These tea bricks were made by compacting tea leaves into a dense block, which could then be easily transported and exchanged for goods and services.

401 Brad Pitt, an American actor, was reportedly banned from China for his role in the 1997 film "7 Years in Tibet." The movie tells the story of the Dalai Lama's escape from Chinese-occupied Tibet, which China deemed as being critical of its actions in Tibet.

402 New York City is known for its bustling coffee culture, and it is often said that New Yorkers drink nearly seven times more coffee than other cities in the United States.

403 Caligynephobia is the fear of beautiful women. This phobia is considered to be a specific phobia and can cause Serious distress and impairment in daily life.

404 The movie "Titanic" won 11 Academy Awards in 1998, but none of the awards were for acting. The film won in categories such as Best Picture, Best Director, and Best Original Song.

405 It is commonly stated that 99% of a panda's diet consists of bamboo. However, pandas will also eat small amounts of fruits, vegetables, and other plants, as well as fish and small mammals.

406 Snakes are responsible for the deaths of approximately 100,000 people each year. But it should be noted that many snake species are not venomous and do not cause a threat to humans.

407 The first soccer game that was televised occurred on May 24, 1937. This match was broadcast by BBC Television and featured the London team Arsenal playing against the London team Arsenal Reserves.

408 The mortality rate of a Black Mamba snake bite is close to 100%. This means that the majority of people who are bitten by a Black Mamba will die as a result of the venom.

409 Ronaldinho, a retired Brazilian professional soccer player, had a sponsorship deal with Coca-Cola. However, this deal ended after he was caught drinking a Pepsi during a news conference.

410 Ancient Egyptians used various remedies for toothaches, including the use of dead mice. This was believed to be an effective method for alleviating pain and inflammation in the affected area.

411 "Rap God" by Eminem is a song that is known for its fast-paced rap style and high word count. The song has 1,560 words making it the song with the most words.

412 California has a larger population than Canada, despite Canada being more than 2,000 percent larger in size than California.

Don't cry in space

413 In space, you can't cry like you do on Earth because there is no gravity to pull the tears down the face. The tears would instead remain in a liquid state and float around the astronaut's face.

414 Spiders are known to eat their own webs in order to recycle the silk, which they use to build new webs. This is a way for them to conserve resources and make the most of the silk they produce.

415 In 1894, Japan offered to buy the Philippines from Spain for 40 million pounds.

416 In 1977, a signal from deep space was received that lasted 72 seconds. This signal, known as the "Wow! Signal," remains a mystery to this day, as the origin of the signal has never been determined.

417 Spider silk is known for its exceptional strength, with some species producing silk that is up to five times stronger than steel of the same weight. This makes spider silk one of the strongest materials known to man, and scientists are currently researching ways to replicate its properties for use in a variety of applications.

418 The United States has a large Spanish-speaking population, with more Spanish speakers than Spain. According to some estimates, there are more than 41 million Spanish speakers in the U.S.

419 Whales, large marine mammals, produce vocalizations known as songs which can be used to study their behavior and the ocean environment. In some cases, these songs can be used to map the ocean floor.

420 The tongue is the only muscle in the body that is attached at one end.

421 William Shakespeare, an English playwright and poet, passed away in 1616, and his remains are buried in Holy Trinity Church, in Stratford-upon-Avon, England.

422 A single cigarette contains a vast array of chemicals, with a total of over 4,800 present in each one. Of these, 69 have been identified as known carcinogens.

423 The Solar System is estimated to be around 4.5 billion years old, formed from a cloud of gas and dust that eventually coalesced to form the Sun and the planets that orbit it.

424 Humans spend a big portion of their lives sleeping, with approximately one-third of their existence devoted to this activity.

425 On a global scale, an astounding 15 billion cigarettes are smoked every day.

426 Benjamin Franklin, one of America's founding fathers, made efforts to abolish slavery as early as 1790.

427 In Russia, the population statistics show that there are approximately 9 million more women than men. This imbalance is thought to be due to a combination of factors, including a higher mortality rate among men and a preference for male children in some cultures.

428 Tomatoes have a higher number of genes than humans. The tomato genome contains approximately 35,000 genes, while the human genome contains approximately 20,000-25,000 genes.

429 The word "vodka" comes from the Russian word "voda," which means "water." Vodka is a clear distilled spirit that is traditionally made from fermented grains or potatoes.

430 Apple Inc. is worth more than the entire Russian stock market. As of 2021, the market capitalization of Apple Inc. was over $2 trillion, while the entire Russian stock market was valued at around $1 trillion.

431 When the moon is directly overhead, the gravitational pull of the moon on an object on the surface of the earth will be stronger, which can make the object weigh slightly less.

432 27,000 trees are felled each day to produce toilet paper. The production of toilet paper requires large amounts of wood pulp, which is obtained by cutting down trees.

433 It is estimated that a large portion of all data in the world, approximately 95%, is still stored on paper. This means that a large amount of information is never accessed or used again after it is initially recorded.

434 Recycling aluminum cans is an important way to save energy. By recycling one aluminum can, enough energy is saved to run a television for two hours.

435 The Central Intelligence Agency (CIA) uses a process called document destruction to dispose of classified documents. One way they do this is by burning the documents to generate heat that is used to warm the water supply for the agency.

436 The smallest bone in the human body is located in the inner ear and is called the stapes or stirrup bone.

437 Bones have the ability to heal themselves through a process called bone remodeling, in which new bone cells are produced to replace damaged or old ones.

438 The human reproductive system contains the smallest and largest cells in the body. The smallest are sperm cells, while the largest are egg cells.

439 The pH level of the vagina is slightly acidic, with a pH range of 3.8 to 4.5, similar to that of tomatoes.

440 Some women are born with two uteruses, a condition known as uterus didelphys.

441 A man can produce more than 500 billion sperm cells in his lifetime.

442. Snails can enter a state of torpor, which is similar to hibernation, and can remain in this state for several months, including up to three years in some species.

443. The oldest recorded woman to give birth is 66 years old.

444. In 2009, Nadya Suleman gave birth to octuplets (6 boys and 2 girls)

445. More than 40% of the human body's weight is made up of muscle tissue.

446. Studies have shown that the rate of heart attacks is higher on Mondays compared to other days of the week.

447. Africa is a continent that spans across all four hemispheres: the northern hemisphere, southern hemisphere, eastern hemisphere, and western hemisphere.

448. Hippopotamus milk is pink in color, unlike most other mammals' milk which is white. The pink color comes from the presence of red blood cells in the milk.

449. New creatures have been discovered in deep-sea hydrothermal vents and cold seeps, which are areas around undersea volcanoes where hot water and chemicals are released. These creatures are able to survive in extreme conditions due to unique adaptations.

450. The word "SWIMS" is still "SWIMS" when turned upside down, this is known as a symmetrical word.

451. The Lego Group is a very popular and well-known brand. There are more Lego Minifigures than there are people on Earth, as the company has produced billions of minifigures.

452. Some perfumes contain ambergris, a waxy substance that is produced in the stomachs of sperm whales and excreted.

453. Psychologists recognize more than 400 distinct phobias, which are intense and irrational fears of specific things or situations.

454 Fruit stickers, also known as produce labels, are small labels that are often placed on fruits and vegetables to identify the type and origin of the product. These labels are made of edible materials and are safe to eat.

455 An astronaut is a person who is trained to travel and work in outer space. The word astronaut is a compound word, which is made up of two Ancient Greek words "astro," meaning "star," and "naut," meaning "sailor."

456 At birth, baby pandas are incredibly small and fragile. They typically weigh between 3 and 5 ounces, which is smaller than the average mouse.

457 The flashes of colored light that you see when you rub your eyes are called "phosphenes." These flashes are caused by the mechanical stimulation of the retina, which leads to the activation of cells in the eye that respond to light.

458 Iceland does not have a railway system. Instead, the country relies on a network of roads and buses to transport people and goods.

459 The largest known prime number is currently known as M77232917. It is a number that has 17,425,170 digits and it was discovered in 2018 by a computer program.

460 Forrest Fenn, an art dealer and author, is said to have hidden a treasure chest in the Rocky Mountains worth over 1 million dollars. The treasure chest has not been found yet, and Fenn's treasure hunt is still ongoing.

461 In Japan, there is a company that offers classes on how to be funny. These classes teach students how to write and deliver jokes, as well as how to improve their comedic timing and delivery. This is a profession that is highly valued in Japan, and is seen as a way to improve one's communication skills.

462 James Cameron, the filmmaker known for directing movies such as Titanic and Avatar, actually worked as a truck driver before starting his career in the film industry as a special effects artist and eventually transitioning to directing.

463 More people are killed each year by bees and hornets than by snakes.

464 In Russia, it is considered a criminal offense to drive a vehicle with a dirty exterior. This rule is enforced by local authorities, who may issue fines or penalties to those found in violation.

465 Bees have been trained to detect certain odors, including those associated with explosives. This is known as "bee odor detection" and is being researched as a potential tool for homeland security and military applications.

466 Research suggests that the type of music a person listens to can influence their perception of the world around them.

467 Blind individuals have never developed schizophrenia, which is a mental disorder characterized by a disconnection from reality.

468 Approximately 3 in every 10 teenage girls in the United States become pregnant. In the United States, it is estimated that 49% of pregnancies are unintended, resulting in the birth of more than 3 million children each year.

469 A large portion of the world's population lives in poverty, with 80% of humanity surviving on less than US$10 per day.

470 In the United States, the poorest area is Allen, South Dakota, where a majority of the population, 96%, are Native American.

471 Modern mobile phones have more computing power than the computers used for the Apollo 11 mission, which was one of the most expensive and technologically advanced projects in history.

472 Monkeys have been observed to have the ability to count, though their level of understanding and use of numbers is limited compared to humans.

473 While the color red is often associated with anger in bulls, it is actually a myth that bulls are angered by the color red. In reality, bulls are color-blind.

Scary culture fact

474 The Aztecs, an ancient Mesoamerican civilization, were known for their human sacrifices. According to historical records, they sacrificed around 1% of their population every year. These sacrifices were believed to appease their gods and ensure the continued prosperity of the Aztec empire.

475 Smoking can lead to impotence, or the inability to achieve or maintain an erection, in men. This is because smoking can damage blood vessels and decrease blood flow to the penis.

476 McDonald's, the fast food giant, did not originally serve hamburgers. When it first opened in 1940, the menu consisted of hot dogs, barbecue, and soft drinks. It wasn't until later that hamburgers were added to the menu.

477 In North Korea, marijuana is not classified as a drug and is legal to use and possess. However, this does not mean that marijuana use is widespread or openly accepted in the country. The possession and use of other drugs, such as heroin and cocaine, is strictly prohibited and punishable by severe penalties.

478 The small cardboard holder, often used to hold takeaway cups of coffee, is known as a "zarf."

479 The Triangle, a percussion instrument, took a long time to gain popularity in orchestral settings. It took nearly 100 years for the instrument to become widely accepted in orchestral performances.

480 Losing weight is a common goal for many people, and is often a New Year's resolution.

481 During World War II, the first bomb dropped on Berlin by the Allies resulted in the death of the only elephant at the Berlin Zoo, which was an unfortunate collateral damage of the war.

482 At the time of his death in 1973, Pablo Picasso was the wealthiest artist in history, having amassed a large fortune through the sale of his works.

483. In New Jersey, it is illegal to wear a bulletproof vest while committing a violent crime, as it can be seen as an indication of intent to commit the crime.

484. A group of whales is referred to as a "pod"

485. Putting your phone in airplane mode can prevent ads from appearing while playing games, as it disables the phone's connection to the internet.

486. The core of the Earth is extremely hot, with temperatures reaching up to 7,200 degrees Fahrenheit, which is as hot as the surface of the sun.

487. Earth is radioactive due to the presence of naturally occurring radioactive elements in the planet's crust and core.

488. Mosses are a type of plant that can be found in many different environments around the world, from forests to deserts. They are able to survive in a wide range of conditions due to their ability to store water and adapt to different climates.

489. According to mathematicians, there are a total of 177,147 ways to tie a tie.

490. Monkeys, like many other animals, have been observed to practice dental hygiene by flossing their teeth. This behavior is believed to be a way for them to remove debris and prevent tooth decay.

491. Flowers have been found to grow faster when exposed to music. Scientists believe that this may be due to the vibrations created by the music, which can stimulate the growth of the plants.

492. Peaches are one of the most widely cultivated fruits in America, and are particularly popular, ranking as the third most popular fruit grown in the country.

493. In North Korea, citizens are only allowed to choose from 28 approved haircuts. This is part of the government's strict control over personal appearance and is believed to be an effort to maintain a certain image of conformity among the population.

494 Dead skin cells are one of the main components of household dust. They can come from people, pets, and even indoor plants, and can contribute to allergies and other respiratory issues.

495 The dry air in an airplane can cause dehydration, which can affect your sense of taste. This can make food and drinks taste differently than they normally would, leading to a decrease in taste bud sensitivity.

496 A bolt of lightning is incredibly hot, with temperatures reaching up to 50,000 degrees Fahrenheit. This is five times hotter than the surface of the sun, which has an average temperature of around 10,000 degrees Fahrenheit.

497 The fastest recorded raindrop was measured to be traveling at a speed of 18 miles per hour. This is due to the force of gravity pulling the raindrop down, as well as wind and air resistance acting on it.

498 PayPal, an electronic payment system, was once considered a poor business idea in 1999. However, the company has since proven to be a successful and widely-used service.

499 Research has shown that a majority of people tend to tilt their heads to the right when kissing someone else. The reason for this behavior is not entirely clear, but it may be related to the way the brain processes visual information.

500 The sensation of a tickle in the throat can be relieved by scratching the ear. This is because the vagus nerve, which runs from the brainstem to the ear, is stimulated by the act of scratching, thus providing relief from the tickling sensation.

501 Tumors are abnormal growths in the body that can take on various forms. Some tumors have been known to produce hair, teeth, bones, and even fingernails, but this is rare and typically indicative of a cancerous tumor.

502 Recent droughts in Europe have been among the worst in recorded history, with some studies suggesting that they may be the worst in 2,100 years.

503 According to a study, 1 in every 8 deaths on Earth is linked to air pollution. Air pollution is caused by the release of harmful particles and gases into the atmosphere and can lead to a wide range of health problems, including respiratory and cardiovascular disease, cancer, and stroke.

504 The original Star Wars film, released in 1977, premiered on just 32 screens across the United States. Despite this limited release, the film went on to become one of the most successful and popular movies of all time.

505 In 2010, Apple paid a couple $1.7 million dollars for their small plot of land, which was only worth $181,700 at the time. The land was located near Apple's headquarters in Cupertino, California and the company planned to use it for a new campus.

506 Brazil is home to the largest Japanese population outside of Japan, with an estimated 1.6 million people of Japanese descent living in the country. This is due to a large number of Japanese immigrants who arrived in Brazil in the early 20th century to work on coffee plantations.

507 Paint was historically stored in pig bladders because they were readily available and provided a flexible, airtight container for the paint. The bladder would be filled with paint and then tied off to seal it. This method of storage was used until more modern containers such as glass jars and metal cans became widely available.

508 It is true that humans have jumped farther than horses in the Olympics, specifically in the long jump event. The current world record for the long jump by a human is 8.95 meters (29 feet 4.5 inches), set by Mike Powell in 1991. In contrast, the longest recorded jump by a horse is 8.04 meters (26 feet 4.5 inches), set by a horse named Huaso in 1949. This is because the human body is built for jumping and running, while horses are built for running and galloping.

509 Russia has a long history of vodka consumption, and it is a cultural staple in the country. It is said that during World War II, the country celebrated the end of the war by consuming large amounts of vodka, which led to a shortage.

510 In 18th century England, pineapples were considered a symbol of wealth and luxury. They were expensive to grow and transport, so only the wealthy could afford to have them in their homes.

511 In 1907, a woman was arrested on a beach in Boston for wearing a one-piece swimsuit. At that time, it was considered scandalous and immodest for women to reveal that much skin in public.

512 Coca-Cola owns a wide range of website URLs that can be read as "ahh" with up to 62 'h's. This is a branding strategy to protect the company's name and prevent others from using similar URLs.

513 Sprite was created by Coca-Cola as a response to the popularity of 7 Up. sprite is a lemon-lime flavored soft drink, similar to 7 Up.

514 The Latin name for banana is "musa sapientum," which translates to "fruit of the wise men." This name is thought to have been given to the banana because it was considered a symbol of knowledge and wisdom in ancient cultures.

515 The human foot contains 26 bones, including those in the toes and heel.

516 It is physically impossible to lick one's own elbow due to the positioning of the elbow joint and the muscles that control the movement of the arm.

517 Carrots were not originally orange. They were originally purple, yellow or white, it was only in the 17th century in Holland that orange carrots were developed.

518 When video game Minecraft was developed, only one of the developers, Markus Persson, had previously worked on a video game before.

519 Sloths have more neck bones than giraffes, with sloths having 7 cervical vertebrae, while giraffes have only 6.

Pythons massage

520 In Jakarta, there is a spa that uses pythons to massage clients. This is not a common practice and it is unclear if it is considered safe or ethical.

521 Johnny Appleseed, also known as John Chapman, was an American pioneer nurseryman who introduced apple trees to large parts of Pennsylvania, Ohio, Indiana, and Illinois, but his apples were not intended for eating. They were planted for cider production and apple orchards.

522 In ancient Rome, people used a sponge on a stick, called a "xylospongium" or "tersorium", to clean themselves after using the toilet. These sponges were often shared among multiple people, which could have led to the spread of disease.

523 Lake Hillier in Western Australia is known for its bright pink color, which is caused by a high concentration of a type of microorganism called Dunaliella salina. Scientists are still studying the lake to understand more about the unique coloration.

524 Albert Einstein's eyes were removed during his autopsy and are kept in a safe deposit box in New York City. This was done at the request of Einstein's son and against the wishes of Einstein himself.

525 Many creatures that live in the deep sea are capable of producing light through a process called bioluminescence. This is thought to be an adaptation that allows them to communicate, attract prey, or evade predators. However, not 90% of all creatures that live underwater, below 1,500 feet, are luminous.

526 Lettuce is a member of the sunflower family, scientifically known as Asteraceae.

527 Honeybees are capable of flying at high altitudes, with some estimates suggesting they can fly as high as 29,500 feet, which is higher than Mount Everest.

528 In the novel Frankenstein, the creature created by Victor Frankenstein is depicted as a vegetarian, refraining from eating meat.

529 Obesity is a major health concern in the United States, with approximately one in three Americans being classified as obese. This can lead to a host of health problems such as diabetes, heart disease, and cancer. It is important for individuals to maintain a healthy diet and exercise regimen to prevent or manage obesity.

530 As of 2021, it is estimated that there are approximately 9 million people in prisons around the world, with an estimated quarter of the world's prison population being held in the US.

531 According to a survey, a significant proportion (33%) of dog owners admitted to having conversations with their dogs over the phone, indicating that they may consider their pets to be social companions.

532 Education is an important factor in the empowerment of women and girls. Girls who complete secondary school are 6 times less likely to become child brides than those who do not receive an education.

533 Whales are long-lived creatures, and scientists have developed a way to determine their age by counting the rings in their earwax. Similar to tree rings, these layers provide an annual record of the whale's growth and can reveal its age.

534 The man with the world's deepest voice can make sounds that are inaudible to humans. This man is capable of producing sounds that are below the range of human hearing.

535 The current American flag was designed by a high school student. A 17-year-old student named Robert G. Heft designed the current U.S. flag as a school project, and it was later adopted as the official flag of the United States.

536 When the oxygen supply is cut off, the brain can survive for a few minutes before brain damage begins to occur. This is due to the brain's ability to store a small amount of oxygen in the blood vessels and use it during a period of oxygen deprivation.

537 Uranus, a gas giant planet in our solar system, has a unique orbital system that leads to extremely long seasons. The summer on Uranus lasts for 42 Earth years, while its winter lasts for an equally long 42 Earth years.

538 The U.S. government's Library of Congress has been saving every public tweet since 2006, with the collection ending in 2017.

539 Giraffes have extremely long tongues, some measuring up to 20 inches in length.

540 When tomatoes were first introduced to Europe, many people were hesitant to eat them because they were thought to be poisonous.

541 Dreaming is not unique to humans and has also been observed in other animals, including primates, birds, and mammals.

542 Percy Spencer, the inventor of the microwave oven, received only $2 as a bonus for his discovery while working at Raytheon Corporation.

543 Saint Lucia is the only country in the world that is named after a woman, specifically Saint Lucy of Syracuse.

544 Scientists have discovered that there are sharks living in an active underwater volcano. However, divers are unable to investigate due to the extreme acidity and heat present in the volcano.

545 In the United States, it is a tradition for children to receive money, usually around $3.70, for each tooth that falls out.

546 The song "I Will Always Love You" was originally written and recorded in 1973 by Dolly Parton. It was later covered by Whitney Houston in 1992.

547 Vanilla flavoring is sometimes made using castoreum, which is a substance obtained from the castor sacs of beavers. It is considered safe for consumption.

548 Newborn babies are not able to see in color for a few months as their eyes are not fully developed, and they can only perceive black and white.

549 Only a quarter of the Sahara Desert is composed of sand dunes; the rest is mostly rocky or gravel terrain.

550 Mercedes-Benz, a German luxury car manufacturer, has developed a concept car that can be controlled using a joystick instead of traditional controls such as a steering wheel and pedals.

551 On average, women spend approximately one year of their lives deciding what to wear, highlighting the societal pressure to present a certain appearance.

552 The hole in the ozone layer over Antarctica is alarmingly large, with its size being twice the area of Europe.

553 Greenhouse gas emissions from the meat consumption of an average U.S. family of four can be higher than those from driving two cars. This is because the production and transportation of meat can release large amounts of carbon dioxide and methane.

554 White blood cells can be seen as small, bright dots when looking at the sky. This is due to the way the cells reflect light, and is not a common occurrence.

555 Anatidaephobia is a rare and unusual fear of the belief that somewhere, somehow, a duck or goose is watching you.

556 In 1945, a rooster named Mike was able to survive for 18 months after his head was cut off. This was due to the presence of a blood clot that prevented blood loss from the severed head.

557 Human saliva contains a natural painkiller called opiorphin which is six times more powerful than morphine.

558 Cows do not have upper front teeth. They have lower incisors and molars on the top jaw, but not upper front teeth.

559 The brain continues to function and process information even during sleep, allowing for important tasks such as memory consolidation and repair.

Cows and climate change

560 In terms of environmental impact, cows are a major contributor to global warming due to their production of methane, which exceeds that of the oil industry.

561 Zebras are able to survive without water for long periods of time, getting the moisture they need from the plants they eat.

562 Every 90 seconds, a woman loses her life during pregnancy or childbirth, a tragic statistic that highlights the ongoing challenges facing maternal health around the world.

563 Research has shown that women tend to use more words than men, with the average woman speaking around 20,000 words per day, compared to the average man's 7,000 words.

564 Most Disney characters wear gloves to keep animation simple. Gloves are worn by many Disney characters as they help to simplify the animation process.

565 The closest living relatives of hippopotamuses are whales, dolphins, and porpoises. This is because they all belong to the order Cetartiodactyla, which also includes other semi-aquatic mammals such as deer, sheep, and goats.

566 There is some research that suggests that people who frequently post about their fitness routines on social media may have a greater likelihood of having psychological issues, such as body dysmorphia or a drive for perfection.

567 There are companies that sell mirrors that are designed to make the person looking in them appear thinner. This is done through optical illusions and special lighting techniques.

568 The abbreviation "Xmas" for Christmas is derived from the Greek letter "X" (chi), which is the first letter of the Greek word "Χριστός" (Christos), meaning "Christ."

569 The symbol "#" is known as the "pound" or "hash" symbol in the United States, "number" in the United Kingdom, and "octothorpe" in some technical contexts.

570 The word "avocado" comes from the Nahuatl (Aztec) word "ahuacatl" which can mean testicle, and it may have been used to refer to the avocado because of its shape.

571 Farts can smell bad due to the presence of certain gases and compounds, such as sulfur, in the intestinal tract.

572 Hiccups occur when the diaphragm, a muscle that helps with breathing, contracts suddenly and involuntarily. This can be caused by factors such as temperature changes or eating too quickly.

573 The Bagheera kiplingi spider is a species of spider that was discovered in the 1800s and is the only species of spider that has been classified as vegetarian, as it primarily feeds on acacia tree leaves.

574 The Roman-Persian Wars were a series of conflicts that occurred between the Roman Empire and the Persian Empire from the 2nd century BC to the 7th century AD. These wars were the longest in history, spanning several centuries.

575 Paraguay's former President, Horacio Cartes was found to be the owner of a stolen car, this was reported by the Paraguayan newspaper ABC Color. However, it is not clear if the President was aware of the car's origins before buying it.

576 Popcorn, a type of corn that expands and puffs up when heated, was first domesticated in Mexico around 9,000 years ago. This ancient form of popcorn was likely used for both consumption and ceremonial purposes.

577 The average McDonald's employee takes around 7 months to earn what the CEO of the company makes in just one hour.

578. Babies blink less frequently than adults, with an average rate of once or twice per minute, while adults blink about 10 times per minute.

579. The human body produces a large amount of saliva, approximately 25,000 quarts, which is enough to fill almost two swimming pools.

580. The lungs are the only organs in the body that have the ability to float on water due to the high air content in the lungs.

581. Coughing and sneezing are natural reflexes that help to remove foreign substances, such as dust or bacteria, from the respiratory system.

582. Children who breathe through their mouths instead of their noses are at a higher risk of developing a lisp when they speak.

583. Earth is a heat engine because it receives energy from the sun, which drives a variety of processes such as weather and ocean currents.

584. Route 66, a famous highway in the United States, is not longer than the distance to the Earth's core. The Earth's core is about 3,000 miles deep, while Route 66 is around 2,500 miles long.

585. Earthquakes can be felt over large distances, but the intensity of shaking decreases with distance from the epicenter.

586. Ed Sheeran is a British singer-songwriter who rose to fame in the early 2010s. According to one story, early in his career, he bought a one-way ticket to Los Angeles with no contacts or connections in the city, in an attempt to break into the music industry.

587. During World War I, Germany established the first service animals, specifically dogs, to assist soldiers with tasks such as detecting and retrieving injured soldiers on the battlefield.

588. Turkeys are able to blush. When they are excited or stressed, blood vessels in their head can become engorged, causing their head to turn red or blue.

The Bermuda Triangle Myth

589 The Bermuda Triangle is a region of the Atlantic Ocean that has been associated with a high number of ship and plane disappearances. However, the number of disappearances in this area is not higher than in any other region of the ocean.

590 Almost a third of San Francisco's air pollution comes from China. This is due to the fact that China is a major producer of goods that are shipped to the United States, and the emissions from these shipping vessels and cargo planes contribute to the air pollution in San Francisco and other nearby cities.

591 Bob Marley's final words are not widely agreed upon, as they were not recorded. Some sources claim that his last words were "Money can't buy life," while others say they were "The people who are trying to make this world worse aren't taking a day off, how can I?"

592 Some octopus species have the ability to lay up to 56,000 eggs at a time. This is a remarkable number of eggs and is a testament to the reproductive capabilities of these creatures.

593 Cats have fewer toes on their back paws than on their front paws. Specifically, they have four toes on their front paws and only three toes on their back paws.

594 Blue whales are able to consume large amounts of food in one mouthful. They are known to eat up to half a million calories in one mouthful.

595 The tiny pocket on jeans was designed to store pocket watches. This pocket, which is typically located inside the larger front pocket, was originally intended for storing pocket watches.

596 Octopuses and squids are cephalopods, a group of marine animals that also includes nautiluses and cuttlefish. These animals have a unique beak-like structure, located at the base of their tentacles, that they use to bite and tear food.

597 In the wild, mice typically have a relatively short lifespan of around six months due to predation and other hazards.

598 Gilberto Baschiera, an Italian banker, is considered a modern-day Robin Hood figure due to his reputation for giving large amounts of money to the poor and needy.

599 Paraguay has a high rate of motorcycle-related accidents, and according to a study conducted by the Paraguay Ministry of Public Health and Social Welfare, 97% of motorcycle riders in the country do not wear helmets.

600 Sugary drinks have been found to be responsible for a large number of deaths in Mexico. In fact, it has been reported that the number of deaths caused by consuming sugary drinks is higher than the number of deaths caused by violent crime in the country.

601 Men are more likely to be struck by lightning than women. Studies have shown that men are five times more likely to be struck by lightning than women. The reasons for this disparity are not entirely clear, but it is thought that men may be more likely to engage in outdoor activities, which would put them at a higher risk of being struck by lightning.

602 Listening to music can have an impact on your heartbeat. Research has shown that the rhythm of your heartbeat can change and mimic the rhythm of the music you are listening to. This suggests that music may have a therapeutic effect on the heart and may be beneficial for people with heart conditions.

603 Many mathematical symbols, such as + and -, were not invented until the 16th century. Prior to that, equations were written in words.

604 The word "forty" is the only number that is spelled with letters arranged in alphabetical order.

605 Over 100,000 people have applied for a one-way trip to colonize Mars in 2022. This is according to Mars One, a private company that plans to establish a permanent human settlement on the red planet.

Funny but true

606 The word "one" is the only number that is spelled with letters arranged in descending order.

607 In North Korea, the ownership of motor vehicles is restricted to military and government officials, while private citizens are not allowed to own them.

608 The nickname "Windy City" for Chicago has nothing to do with the city's weather but rather it is thought to have originated in the 19th century as a reference to the city's long-winded politicians.

609 Mount Everest, the highest peak in the world, experienced a slight reduction in height as a result of the devastating earthquake that struck Nepal in 2015. According to reports, the mountain shrank by one inch as a result of the seismic activity.

610 Peanuts are not actually nuts but rather legumes, a type of plant that grows in the ground.

611 Firefighters use special chemicals called wetting agents to make water even more effective at extinguishing fires by reducing the surface tension of the water and allowing it to penetrate deeper into the fuel source.

612 The days on Earth are getting longer due to the slowing of the Earth's rotation. This is caused by the gravitational pull of the Moon and the Sun on the Earth's oceans, which creates a drag on the Earth's rotation.

613 The continents on Earth have not always been in their current positions. Over millions of years, the continents have moved and collided with each other due to the movement of tectonic plates.

614 The gravity on Earth is not uniform, meaning it is not the same in all parts of the planet. Factors such as the Earth's rotation and the distribution of mass can affect gravity.

615 More people in the world are suffering from obesity than from hunger. According to the World Health Organization, obesity is now considered a global epidemic, with more than 1.9 billion adults and 38 million children under the age of five being classified as overweight or obese.

616 Martin Luther King Jr. was a civil rights leader who fought for equality and justice for African Americans in the United States. He is best known for his role in the American Civil Rights Movement and his speeches, such as "I have a dream". He was arrested 29 times for his activism.

617 In New Zealand, Sign Language is one of the three official languages of the country. This means that it is given equal status to English and Maori and is used in government and other official contexts.

618 Pandas eat bamboo largely because they have no umami taste receptors. Umami is a taste sensation that is often described as savory or meaty, and is present in many foods such as meats, mushrooms, and soy sauce. Pandas, however, lack this receptor, making bamboo a more appealing food source for them.

619 McDonald's experimented with a variety of unusual flavors for their broccoli, including bubblegum.

620 Certain types of fungi are known to infect insects and other organisms, altering their behavior and effectively turning them into "zombies" under the fungus's control.

621 The oranges that were originally cultivated were not the same color as the oranges we know today, but rather a different color like green or yellow.

622 The story of an apple hitting Isaac Newton on the head and inspiring his theory of gravity is a popular anecdote, but it is not supported by historical evidence. Newton's development of the theory of gravity was the result of extensive scientific study and mathematical calculations.

623 Cats are known for their tendency to sleep for prolonged periods of time, with estimates suggesting that they spend as much as 70% of their lives in a state of slumber.

624 In the United States alone, there are over 8.6 million people living with serious illnesses caused by smoking.

625 It is a little-known fact that the first slave owner in America was a black man.

626 Giraffes have a unique sleeping pattern, requiring only 5 to 30 minutes of sleep in a 24-hour period.

627 The Trans-Siberian Railway is a network of railways that connects Moscow to the Russian Far East and the Sea of Japan. It is known for its long distance of 9,258 kilometers and during the trip, travelers will cross over 3901 bridges.

628 Wally Amos is a businessman who is known for creating the Famous Amos chocolate chip cookie brand. He is not just known for his cookies but also for being a motivational speaker and literacy advocate.

629 Dogs have a strong sense of magnetoreception, which allows them to align their bodies with Earth's magnetic field. This is why dogs tend to orient themselves along a north-south axis when going to the bathroom.

630 Colorado, USA is home to an active volcano that last erupted around the same time as the construction of the pyramids in Egypt.

631 It's a common assumption that the average person spends a significant amount of their life waiting at traffic lights. But this statement is not supported by scientific evidence, as the amount of time varies depending on factors such as location, time of day, and one's individual travel patterns.

632 Samsung uses a robot shaped like a human buttocks to test the durability of its phones by simulating the stress of sitting on them.

633 The cornea, the clear outer layer of the eye, is one of the few parts of the human body that does not have blood vessels. This allows light to pass through and reach the retina, which is responsible for sending visual information to the brain.

634 In 1907, the world's first animated feature film, "El Apóstol," was produced in Argentina by cartoonist Quirino Cristiani.

635 German chocolate cake is a type of chocolate cake that is traditionally made with a specific type of sweet chocolate called German chocolate. However, it is not actually from Germany, it was invented in Texas by an American baker named Sam German in the 1850s.

636 Sea levels are projected to rise by up to 2.5 feet by 2100 due to the melting of ice sheets and glaciers, as well as thermal expansion caused by warming oceans.

637 Clouds play a crucial role in regulating Earth's temperature by reflecting incoming solar radiation back into space and trapping outgoing thermal radiation.

638 The origin of the name "Earth" is uncertain. It is believed to have been derived from the Old English word "ertha," which means ground or soil.

639 In the past, professional athletes would participate in vaudeville performances during the off-season to supplement their income.

640 Astronauts in space may experience a temporary change in height due to changes in spinal alignment caused by the lack of gravity. However, the change is typically less than 2 inches.

641 Scientists predict that the Earth's ozone layer, which protects us from harmful ultraviolet radiation, will fully recover in about 50 years due to a decrease in the use of ozone-depleting chemicals.

642 While it has not been proven yet, some scientists believe that the soil on Mars could be particularly good for growing asparagus. This is due to the presence of certain mineral compounds in the soil, which are thought to be similar to those found in asparagus on Earth.

643 In Paraguay, the longest hot dog ever made was recorded in a festival. The hot dog was measured over 100 meters long and was made with traditional Paraguayan ingredients.

644 Penguins are known to spend about half of their time on land and half in the oceans. They use their time on land to breed and raise their young, and then spend the rest of their time in the ocean foraging for food.

645 According to statistics, Americans make up about 5% of the world's population, but they produce a large amount of waste and consume a large portion of the world's resources. In particular, it is estimated that Americans produce around 30% of the world's waste and use 25% of the world's resources.

646 It takes about 90 days for a drop of water to travel the entire length of the Mississippi River, from its source in Minnesota to the Gulf of Mexico, due to the river's large size and slow-moving water.

647 In the past, some people believed that eating small amounts of arsenic could improve their skin. However, this is not only false but also dangerous, as arsenic is a toxic substance that can cause serious health problems if consumed in large amounts.

648 Penguins, the flightless birds that are native to Antarctica and other southern regions, have a special organ near their eyes that helps them filter salt out of the water they drink. This allows them to drink seawater without suffering from the negative effects of high salt content.

649 Australia has the highest number of venomous snakes in the world.

650 Sharks are responsible for an average of 12 human deaths per year. However, it is important to note that the vast majority of shark species are not dangerous to humans and attacks are relatively rare.

651 Sharks do have an excellent sense of smell, which they use for hunting and navigation. They can detect a single drop of blood in a large body of water, and can even locate prey buried in the sand.

652 Sharks have the ability to regrow their teeth. Depending on the species, sharks can grow a new set of teeth in a matter of days or weeks. In some species, such as the sand tiger shark, new teeth are already in place and ready to replace lost teeth.

653 Nelson Mandela was the first black President of South Africa, serving from 1994-1999. He played a crucial role in ending the system of apartheid in the country and promoting racial reconciliation.

654 It is believed that Isaac Newton, the famous scientist and mathematician, died a virgin. He is known for his work in physics, optics, and mathematics, including the development of calculus.

655 South Africa's history of colonialism and apartheid has led to a significant disparity in land ownership, with white people currently owning 72% of the country's farmland, even though they make up only 8% of the population.

656 Glaciers and ice sheets hold about 69 percent of the world's freshwater. This water is stored in the form of ice and snow, and is an important resource for many communities around the world.

657 In 1964, there was a soccer match between Argentina and Peru in which a controversial refereeing decision led to a riot among fans, in which over 300 people were killed.

The largest animal in the world

658 The blue whale is the largest animal in the world and is known for its massive size. One of the most striking features of the blue whale is its heart, which can be as large as a car.

659 Elephants are known for their long pregnancy, which can last for up to 2 years. This is one of the longest pregnancies in the animal kingdom and is necessary to ensure that the elephant's offspring is fully developed and able to survive in the wild.

660 The Apollo 11 mission was the first successful manned mission to land on the Moon. The mission was a historic achievement and was a major milestone in space exploration. However, it was also a risky endeavor, and the Apollo 11 spacecraft had only about 20 seconds of fuel left when it landed on the moon.

661 The national anthem of Spain, "La Marcha Real," is unique, it has no official lyrics. It is one of the few national anthems in the world without words.

662 The Korean Demilitarized Zone (DMZ) is often considered to be the world's most militarized zone, as it separates North and South Korea and has a high military presence on both sides.

663 Mercury, the only metal that is liquid at standard room temperature and pressure.

664 Japan has a huge number of vending machines, with roughly one machine for every 40 people.

665 The word "period" was not commonly used on television to refer to menstruation until 1985.

666 The longest English word is 189,819 letters long. This word, which is a chemical name, is considered the longest word in the English language.

667 If all of the tweets sent in a single day were printed in a book, it would fill a book with around 10 million pages.

668 Many dinosaurs are only known from a limited amount of fossil evidence, such as a single tooth or bone. This can make it challenging for scientists to fully understand their characteristics and behavior.

669 The Platbos Forest, located in South Africa, is home to a 6000-year-old tree that has a bar inside. The tree is a yellowwood and is considered to be one of the oldest trees in the world.

670 South Korea has one of the lowest birth rates in the world and it has been projected that if the current trend continues, the population of South Koreans will go extinct by 2750.

671 There are species of ants that engage in a practice known as "enslavement," in which they take control of and exploit other colonies of ants for their own benefit.

672 Pluto, the dwarf planet that is located in the outer reaches of our solar system, has ice made out of water on its surface. The ice is thought to be formed by the freezing of atmospheric gases, such as nitrogen and methane, onto the surface of the planet. Additionally, Pluto has a blue sky. But it is not a common.

673 The longest pregnancy on record in humans is 375 days, it is extremely rare and not typical, most pregnancies last between 37 to 42 weeks. This long pregnancy could be due to various factors such as multiple gestations, miscalculation of due date or medical conditions.

674 On average, around 350,000 tweets are sent every minute, according to data from Twitter. This equates to over 500 million tweets per day and over 200 billion tweets per year. This number has likely grown since that time.

675 Spiders have the unique ability to walk on water, because of a phenomenon called surface tension. This is due to the combination of their small size and their hairy legs, which help to distribute their weight evenly across the surface of the water. Additionally, some species of spiders are able to breathe under water by trapping air bubbles against their body.

676 The Queen of the United Kingdom is technically the legal owner of one-sixth of the Earth's land surface, as a result of the laws of succession and the Crown's role as a legal entity. This includes land in countries such as Canada, Australia, and New Zealand, as well as various islands and territories around the world. However, the Queen does not have any practical control over this land.

677 Slavery was not made a statutory offense in the United Kingdom until April 6, 2010, with the passing of the Coroners and Justice Act. Prior to this, it was technically still possible for individuals to be charged with slavery-related offenses under other laws, but there was no specific legislation addressing slavery itself.

678 In 2013, a fake tweet from the Associated Press's Twitter account claimed that there had been explosions at the White House, causing a temporary panic and resulting in a huge drop in the stock market, with an estimated $130 billion wiped off the value of S&P 500 companies.

679 Lemons are denser than water, so they float, while limes are less dense and will sink.

680 The snow on Venus is not made of the same material as snow on Earth. It is theorized that it is made of metal particles, specifically sulfuric acid.

681 Only two countries, Nicaragua and Dominica, use purple as a color in their national flags.

682 U.S. eggs are illegal to be sold in Britain because they are washed before being packaged, a practice that is not allowed in the EU, while British eggs are illegal in the U.S. because they are not washed before packaging, which is a requirement in the U.S. This is a food safety measure in both countries.

Mobile Phones > Toilet

683 In recent years, the number of mobile phone users worldwide has surpassed the number of people with access to toilets. According to the World Health Organization, around 4.8 billion people have access to mobile phones, while around 4.2 billion people have access to improved sanitation facilities. This highlights the rapid pace of technological advancement and the disparity in access to basic necessities between developed and developing countries.

684 Even on Mount Everest, the highest point on Earth, there is high-speed internet available for climbers and researchers, allowing them to stay connected even in the most remote and inhospitable environments.

685 The Titanic's fourth funnel was not a functional part of the ship, but rather was added for aesthetic reasons. The fourth funnel was built to make the ship look more powerful and symmetrical, as it was intended to be a symbol of luxury and opulence. However, it was not necessary for the ship's operation.

686 A tiger's roar is a powerful and distinctive sound that can be heard from a distance of up to 1.8 miles (3 km) away. This is due to the unique structure of a tiger's vocal cords and larynx, which allow them to produce loud, low-frequency sounds that can carry over long distances.

687 Fingertips develop in the embryonic stage of human development, along with other parts of the body.

688 Teratomas are a type of tumor that can contain a variety of tissue types, including hair and teeth. However, these tumors are rare and do not typically form these structures in a functional way.

689 The first recorded car accident took place in Ohio in 1891, marking the beginning of a new era of transportation and the potential for traffic accidents.

690 Benjamin Franklin, one of the founding fathers of the United States and a prolific inventor, chose not to patent any of his numerous innovations.

691 In Sri Lanka, there is a pilgrimage site that is considered sacred by followers of four different religions: Hinduism, Islam, Buddhism, and Christianity. This site is revered for its "sacred footprint," which is believed by each of these religions.

692 Indonesia has a problem with deforestation, and is indeed one of the world's leading countries in terms of deforestation rates. However, it is not necessarily accurate to say that it has the highest rate of deforestation, as this ranking can change from year to year. Additionally, Brazil is also a major contributor to global deforestation, and its rate of deforestation is considered to be among the highest in the world.

693 The inventor of Vaseline, Robert Chesebrough, did claim to eat a spoonful of Vaseline every day as a way of promoting the product. However, this practice is not recommended and there is no scientific evidence to support the health benefits of consuming petroleum jelly.

694 As a young boy, Adolf Hitler had aspirations to become a priest. However, he later went on to lead Germany as Chancellor and Führer during World War II.

695 In India, there is a man who is the head of the world's largest family, with 39 wives and 94 children who all reside together.

696 The fastest gust of wind ever recorded on Earth was 253 miles per hour, which is an extremely high speed and can cause significant damage to buildings and infrastructure.

697 The statue and imagery commonly associated with the Buddha is actually a representation of the historical Buddha, Siddhartha Gautama, rather than an actual physical depiction of him.

698 In 2006, the FBI reportedly planted an informant pretending to be a radical Muslim in a mosque in order to gather intelligence on potential terrorist activities. The Muslims in the mosque reportedly grew suspicious of the informant and reported him to the FBI. This incident sparked criticism from civil rights groups who argued that the FBI's actions violated the rights of the individuals in the mosque.

699. Uranus is a massive planet, with a diameter of approximately 50,724 km, making it the third-largest planet in our solar system. It is so large that 63 Earths could fit inside it.

700. A rat can survive longer without water than a camel. Camels can survive for up to several weeks without water, while rats can survive for several months due to their ability to metabolize food into water.

701. The domain name "cars.com" was sold for a record-breaking amount of $872.3 million.

702. Heroin was first synthesized in 1874 by the German chemist Friedrich Sertürner, and was initially marketed as a treatment for people addicted to morphine. However, it was soon discovered that heroin was itself highly addictive and its use as a medication was discontinued.

703. The United States is one of the largest military powers in the world, so, a large portion of taxes paid by citizens goes towards defense. It is estimated that around 1 in every 5 dollars paid in taxes in the United States goes to defense.

704. Extreme starvation can cause the brain to start to consume its own nerve cells, which can lead to cognitive impairment.

705. Humans are generally slightly taller in the morning than in the evening due to the natural compression of the spine during the day.

706. It is not possible to breathe and swallow simultaneously as the act of swallowing involves closing off the airway to prevent food from entering the lungs.

707. Stomach acid, also known as gastric acid, is a hydrochloric acid that is produced in the stomach to aid in the digestion of food. It is so strong that it can even dissolve metal and can cause burns on the skin if it comes into contact with it.

708. The word "volcano" has its origins in the Roman language, it is derived from the name of the Roman god of fire, Vulcan.

709 Uranus was the first planet discovered with a telescope. It was discovered by Sir William Herschel in 1781.

710 "In ancient Ireland, it was customary for subordinate chieftains to pay homage to their superiors by performing the act of 'sucking the king's nipples,' which symbolized their submission and loyalty."

711 Indonesia is the largest island country in the world, boasting over 13,000 islands and a rich cultural heritage.

712 Nikola Tesla was known to have a aversion to pearls, and would avoid wearing or handling them whenever possible.

713 In 1903, Thomas Edison sought to discredit the work of Nikola Tesla by publicly electrocuting an elephant using Tesla's alternating current (AC) technology, which he claimed was dangerous.

714 India is the world's largest democracy, with over 1.3 billion people eligible to participate in the democratic process through regular elections.

715 In Indonesia, there is a volcano that is known for its unusual blue flames that spew from its crater.

716 Horses are able to sleep standing up, which is a useful adaptation for animals that need to be ready to flee from predators at a moment's notice.

717 Heart disease is the leading cause of death for women worldwide, accounting for more deaths than all forms of cancer combined.

718 The average human will yawn approximately 250,000 times over the course of their lifetime. Yawning is a natural reflex that helps regulate our breathing and oxygen levels. It is also believed to play a role in our brain's cooling system and can be contagious, with people often yawning in response to others doing so. As we age, our average body temperature tends to decrease.

719. According to research, it is estimated that between 10 to 20 volcanoes are erupting somewhere on Earth on a daily basis. This is due to the planet's active geology and plate tectonics.

720. The Vietnam War was a prolonged conflict that took place in Vietnam, Laos, and Cambodia from 1955 to 1975. One of the tactics employed during this war was the use of snipers. Snipers were trained to crawl across open fields and take out high-value targets. There are stories of a Vietnam War sniper who is said to have crawled for 3 days across 2000 meters of open field, killed a general with one shot, and then crawled back to safety.

721. U.S. troops in Vietnam employed over 5,000 'war dogs' which were trained to detect enemy soldiers, locate booby traps and mines, and track down wounded soldiers.

722. It is estimated that around 80% of volcanic eruptions happen underwater, primarily in the oceanic crust around the Earth's mid-oceanic ridges. These eruptions can create new seafloor, and can form volcanic islands and seamounts.

723. During the Vietnam War, the U.S. dropped more than 2 million tons of bombs on Laos from 1964 to 1973. This is equivalent to a planeload every 8 minutes for 9 years. This bombing campaign was an attempt to disrupt enemy supply lines and infrastructure, but it also had devastating consequences for the civilian population of Laos.

724. Exposure to second-hand smoke, also known as passive smoking, can have significant health consequences. According to the U.S. Surgeon General, it is responsible for nearly 50,000 deaths each year in the United States alone. This can include lung cancer, heart disease, and respiratory illnesses.

725. Angel Falls, located in Venezuela, is one of the world's tallest waterfalls. It stands at a height of 3,212 feet (979 meters), which is over 17 times taller than Niagara Falls. This natural wonder is a popular tourist destination and is considered one of Venezuela's most iconic landmarks.

726. Baby elephants use their trunks to suckle from their mothers.

727 The blue whale is the largest animal on earth, and its mouth can hold an incredible amount of water. In fact, the weight of the water in a blue whale's mouth can be as much as its entire body weight.

728 World War 1 was a global conflict that lasted from 1914 to 1918, and it involved many soldiers from different countries. One interesting fact is that the youngest soldier to serve during WW1 was only 8 years old.

729 Whaling has been a practice for many centuries, but in the 20th century, the number of whales killed increased dramatically. It is estimated that humans killed at least 2.8 million whales in the 20th century.

730 Today, the levels of CO_2 in the atmosphere are higher than they have been in the last 800,000 years, a disturbing trend that has major implications for our planet's future.

731 In Talkeetna, Alaska, a cat named Stubbs has served as the honorary mayor for 15 years. The town does not have a human mayor, and Stubbs was elected through a write-in campaign by the residents.

732 The venom of the boomslang snake can cause a person to bleed from all openings in the body, including the nose, mouth, and eyes. This is because the venom affects the blood clotting process, leading to excessive bleeding.

733 Flamingos are known for their pink coloration, which is due to a pigment called beta-carotene found in the algae and crustaceans, such as shrimp, that they eat.

734 Honeybees have been shown to be able to learn and recognize human faces using visual cues, such as facial features and patterns of movement.

735 Goldfish have been found to be able to differentiate between different composers' music. They were trained to associate food with certain compositions, and later they responded to the music they heard.

736 Male kangaroos have been observed to flex their biceps to impress females during courtship.

737. The United States is known for its love of pizza, with an estimated 100 acres of pizza being served every day. This equates to roughly 350 slices per second.

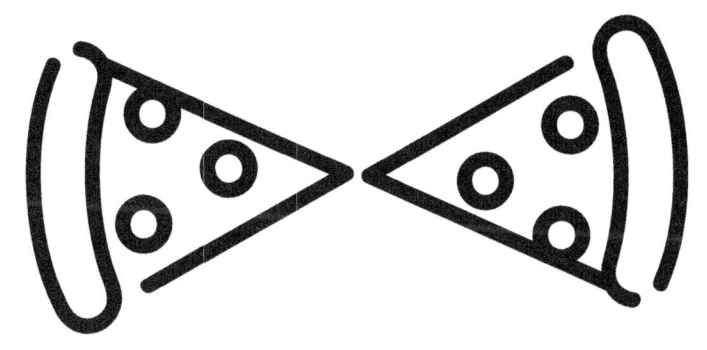

738. During the era of Prohibition in the United States (1920-1933), the government poisoned industrial alcohol to prevent it from being consumed as a recreational beverage. This policy resulted in the deaths of over 10,000 people, as the poisoned alcohol was often sold to unsuspecting consumers.

739. Pork rinds, also known as pork cracklings, were a popular snack during the Renaissance period. They were made by boiling or roasting pork skin, and were considered a cheap and readily available source of protein.

740. Egyptian mummies were wrapped in multiple layers of linen bandages that were often coated in resin to preserve the body. The bandages used to wrap a mummy could stretch up to 1.6 km in length, depending on the size of the body and the number of layers used.

741. According to the 2019 World Happiness Report, Finland is considered to be the world's happiest country.

742. During the late 20th century, around 40% of the world's population lived under Marxist governments.

743. An IKEA store in the Netherlands had to stop offering a one euro breakfast special due to the overwhelming number of customers it attracted and the resulting traffic congestion on the highway.

744. Stephen Hawking, a renowned theoretical physicist, proposed that black holes are not actually black, and that they emit radiation, known as Hawking radiation.

745 Studies have found that human pollution can affect the average length of polar bears' penises, causing them to shrink. Pollutants can disrupt the endocrine system and lead to a decrease in testosterone levels.

746 The liver of a polar bear is highly toxic to humans because it contains a very high level of vitamin A. Eating just a small amount of it can cause acute vitamin A poisoning, which can lead to symptoms such as nausea, vomiting, and even death.

747 Tsutomu Yamaguchi was a Japanese man who survived both atomic bombings in Hiroshima and Nagasaki, as he was in both cities for work related reasons. He is one of the very few recognized double hibakusha (atomic bomb survivors).

748 Stanislawa Leszczynska was a Polish midwife who worked at the Auschwitz concentration camp and helped deliver over 3,000 babies, despite the harsh conditions of the camp.

749 Bananas contain a small amount of a naturally occurring radioactive isotope called potassium-40. However, the amount is so small that it poses no health risk.

750 Despite overwhelming scientific evidence, a big portion of the American population, 37%, believe that global warming is not a real phenomenon.

751 It has been found that the average woman in the UK has 19 pairs of shoes in her collection, but only wears 7 of them regularly.

752 Bacteria can thrive in many different environments, and a study has found that the average office desk has 400 times more bacteria than a toilet seat.

753 Australia's Highway 1 is the longest national highway in the world, stretching over 14,000 kilometers and connecting major cities and towns across the country.

754 As global temperatures continue to rise, flowers are producing less scent.

755 Diabetes is a condition where the body is unable to properly regulate blood sugar levels. One symptom of uncontrolled diabetes is the presence of glucose in the urine, which can give the urine a sweet smell.

756 Your bones contain a significant amount of water, but the percentage may vary depending on your age and overall health. On average, bones are about 31% water.

757 Caterpillars have six simple eyes, also known as ocelli, which are located on the top of their head. These eyes are used for light detection and to help the caterpillar orient itself.

758 Monkeys, like many other animals, can experience hair loss as they age. This can be due to a variety of factors, including hormonal changes and stress.

759 The female hummingbird builds the world's smallest bird's nest, which is typically only about the size of a thimble. Despite its small size, the nest is able to securely hold and protect the hummingbird's eggs and young.

760 The homing pigeon, named "Cher Ami," was used during World War I by the U.S. Army Signal Corps to deliver messages between units. During a battle in 1918, the pigeon delivered a message that helped save 194 soldiers who were trapped behind enemy lines.

761 In 2015, Venezuela experienced one of the highest inflation rates in the world, reaching a staggering 141%. This led to an economic instability and hardship for many citizens.

762 The White House, the official residence of the President of the United States, was built by both free and enslaved individuals. The construction of the White House began in 1792 and was completed in 1800. The enslaved individuals who worked on the construction were owned by James Hoban, the Irish-born architect who designed the building.

763 Zebras have a symbiotic relationship with oxpeckers, which feed on the bugs and parasites on their skin and help to keep them clean.

764 Sexual assault is a serious problem in the United States, and the criminal justice system often fails to hold perpetrators accountable. It is estimated that 97% of rapists in the United States never spend a day in jail for their crime.

765 The Pentagon, the headquarters of the United States Department of Defense, has reportedly developed a plan to address the potential threat of a zombie apocalypse. The plan, called CONOP 8888.

766 In 2007, Iran's Revolutionary Guard announced that they had arrested 14 squirrels on suspicion of espionage. The squirrels were reportedly found near the Iranian-Azerbaijan border, and the Guard claimed that they were being used to gather intelligence by foreign powers.

767 Mahatma Gandhi, the leader of the Indian independence movement, was nominated for the Nobel Peace Prize five times between 1937 and 1948, but he never won the award. He was assassinated in 1948.

768 Nigeria has a larger population of English speakers than the United Kingdom, as it was a former British colony and English is one of the official languages. However, the United Kingdom has a higher percentage of its population that speaks English as a first language.

769 The stripes on a tiger's coat are unique, much like human fingerprints. Each tiger has its own distinct pattern of stripes, which can be used to identify individual animals for research and conservation purposes.

770 It is reported that the CIA reads up to 5 million tweets a day as a part of their open-source intelligence gathering. This allows them to track global events and identify potential security threats.

771 Sweden offers a monthly stipend of SEK 1,500 (approximately US$187) to students attending high school. It is intended to provide financial assistance to students who cannot afford the costs associated with attending school.

772 Access to clean and safe drinking water is a critical issue around the world, with more than 1 billion people still lacking access to fresh water.

773. In Sweden, it is legal to abort a child based on its gender. This is a controversial issue and some argue that it should be illegal as it discriminates against a specific group of individuals.

774. The use of energy-efficient lightbulbs can have a important impact on energy consumption and costs worldwide. If everyone switched to energy-efficient bulbs, it is estimated that the world would save around US$120 billion annually. This is due to the fact that these bulbs use less energy than traditional incandescent bulbs, which can lower energy costs and reduce the need for additional power generation.

775. Plants are able to convert sunlight into energy through the process of photosynthesis. On a daily basis, plants are able to produce energy equivalent to six times the entire power consumption of human civilization.

776. Energy production and consumption are major contributors to climate change, accounting for around 60% of total global greenhouse gas emissions. This is primarily due to the burning of fossil fuels such as coal, oil, and natural gas. Therefore, reducing energy consumption and increasing the use of renewable energy sources can play a critical role in addressing climate change.

777. In Sweden, there are certain restrictions on what you can name your child. For example, you cannot give your child a name that would cause offense or that could be considered to be too commercial. This means that names such as "Ikea" and "Elvis" would not be allowed.

778. The sun is one of the most perfectly round natural objects known to exist in the universe. This is due to the fact that it is primarily composed of plasma and is not solid. The force of gravity keeps it from collapsing and spinning faster, as a result, it has a uniform shape. The sun's roundness is often used as a measure of other celestial bodies' roundness as well.

779. It is a sad fact that every 40 seconds, someone around the world takes their own life. Suicide is a complex issue that can be caused by a variety of factors, including mental health conditions, relationship problems, financial stress, and more.

780 The shortest war in history was the Anglo-Zanzibar War in 1896, which lasted only 38 minutes. The conflict took place between the United Kingdom and the Zanzibar Sultanate and resulted in the British taking control of the island.

781 Glass balls may appear to bounce higher than rubber ones because they are more transparent, making it easier to see the height of their bounces. However, this is an optical illusion, as the height of a bounce depends on the elasticity of the ball and not its material.

782 A tsunami can travel at speeds comparable to that of a jet plane. Tsunamis are massive ocean waves that are generated by underwater earthquakes, volcanic eruptions, and other underwater events. They can travel across the open ocean at speeds of up to 700 km/h, which is faster than a typical commercial jet plane.

783 The world's quietest room is located at Orfield Laboratories in Minnesota, United States. The room, known as the "anechoic chamber," is designed to be acoustically silent, with soundproof walls and a floor that absorbs all sound waves.

784 It is estimated that four babies are born every second worldwide. This means that the global population is growing at a rapid pace, with millions of new births every year.

785 Japan is considered one of the most earthquake-prone countries in the world, due to its location on the Pacific Ring of Fire. The country experiences many earthquakes each year, some of which can be very strong and cause widespread damage.

786 The number of bacteria on Earth is estimated to be around 4 quadrillion quadrillion (4 with 16 zeros). This means that there are more bacteria on our planet than there are stars in the observable universe. Bacteria play a crucial role in many ecological and biochemical processes, and they can be found in a wide range of environments, from soil to water to the human gut.

787 The female lion plays a crucial role in hunting, being responsible for approximately 90% of the prey brought back to the pride.

788 Although he is primarily remembered as one of the greatest American presidents, Abraham Lincoln was also a skilled wrestler. In fact, he was so accomplished that he was enshrined in the Wrestling Hall of Fame, having lost just one match in more than 300.

789 London is renowned for its diversity, with over 300 different languages being spoken among its residents. This cosmopolitan city is home to people from all over the world, making it one of the most culturally rich and diverse cities on the planet.

790 Cuddling has been scientifically shown to have a similar effect on the brain as taking painkillers. When we hug or cuddle with someone we love, our bodies release oxytocin, a hormone that helps to relieve pain and reduce stress.

791 There is a growing body of research indicating that marijuana is less harmful than both alcohol and tobacco. While all substances have the potential for harm, numerous studies have shown that marijuana is associated with fewer negative health consequences compared to alcohol and tobacco.

792 According to a survey, 2% of couples reported falling in love in a supermarket. While this may seem like a small number, it is worth noting that falling in love can happen anywhere and at any time, and there is no one right way for it to occur.

793 Human life expectancy has seen a significant increase in recent years, especially over the last 50 years. Advances in medical technology, improved access to healthcare, and healthier lifestyles have all contributed to a higher average lifespan for people worldwide.

794 In the 19th century, one tiger alone was responsible for killing 430 people in Nepal and India.

795 The Simpsons is one of the longest-running animated television series, with over 700 episodes produced to date. The show has also featured an impressive number of guest stars, with many well-known actors, musicians, and other celebrities making appearances over the years.

796 A very small fraction of the sun is composed of gold, approximately 6×10^{-10}, which is equivalent to 0.0000000006 or one part in 16,666,666,666. This is a minuscule amount and not enough for mining or commercial use.

797 It is predicted that by 2050, Islam will have approximately the same number of followers as Christianity.

798 Right-handed individuals tend to chew their food on the right side of their mouth, while left-handed individuals tend to chew on the left.

799 The Mona Lisa, painted by Leonardo da Vinci, became famous worldwide after it was stolen from the Louvre in 1911. Prior to the theft, it was not widely known.

800 "The current era is considered to be one of the most peaceful periods in human history, despite ongoing conflicts and acts of violence in various parts of the world."

801 "At the age of 4, Adolf Hitler was saved from drowning by a priest, an event that may have had an impact on the course of his life."

802 "Exposure to the air pollution in Mumbai, India, can be equivalent to smoking 100 cigarettes in just one day, highlighting the need for immediate action to improve the city's air quality."

803 "During the Holocaust, an estimated 1.1 million Jewish children were murdered, representing a devastating loss of life and a dark chapter in human history."

804 "Hinduism is a diverse religion that recognizes a vast pantheon of gods and demigods, numbering in the tens of millions."

805 Studies have shown that being in love can have a significant impact on a person's level of productivity. While it can bring joy and a sense of fulfillment, it can also result in decreased focus and attention to tasks and responsibilities.

806. Owls have eyes that are fixed in their sockets, and therefore cannot move them. Instead, they have to move their head to change their field of view.

807. Sea lions are known for their ability to clap to a beat. This is because sea lions have a unique ability to synchronize their movements to music or other rhythmic sounds.

808. Cats have a limited ability to taste sweet flavors. This is because they lack the specific receptor on their tongue that is responsible for detecting sweetness.

809. Coyotes have highly developed auditory abilities and can hear the movement of small animals, such as mice, even when they are buried under several inches of snow.

810. After death, the body begins to decompose. One of the first things that happens is that enzymes that once helped to digest food begin to break down the body's tissues. This process can happen quickly, and within just three days of death, the body may begin to show signs of decomposition.

811. In 2012, more U.S. soldiers died by suicide than in combat. This is a sobering statistic that highlights the importance of addressing mental health issues in the military. Many soldiers who return from combat are at risk for post-traumatic stress disorder (PTSD) and other mental health conditions that can lead to suicide.

812. An ostrich is a large bird that is known for its speed and its ability to run at high speeds. However, it is also known for having a relatively small brain. In fact, an ostrich's eye is actually larger than its brain.

813. It's a common misconception that kissing can lead to tooth decay. While a passionate kiss may temporarily soften the enamel on your teeth, it is unlikely to cause any long-term damage. Tooth decay is typically caused by a combination of factors, such as poor oral hygiene and a high intake of sugary foods.

814. A single bolt of lightning is an extremely powerful force, containing enough energy to instantly toast over 160,000 slices of bread.

815 Italy is recognized globally as the leading producer of wine. The country's rich heritage and favorable climate conditions contribute to its production of some of the world's finest wines.

816 In Japan, the number of pets exceeds the number of children, making pet ownership a popular and common practice in the country.

817 Koalas are known to hug trees to regulate their body temperature on hot days, as the tree provides a cool and shaded environment for them to rest.

818 It is widely believed that the Italian Mafia plays a big role in the country's economy, with some estimates suggesting that it may account for 7% of Italy's GDP.

819 Despite being a minority in the general population, 40% of individuals diagnosed with schizophrenia are known to be left-handed.

820 Over the course of an average lifetime, human skin completely replaces itself approximately 900 times, as old skin cells are naturally shed and replaced by new ones.

821 The Jewish population worldwide is roughly the same as the margin of error in China's census.

822 There is an unoccupied spot near the tomb of Muhammad, Islam's prophet, which is reserved for Jesus.

823 Despite the conclusion of World War II, Japan and Russia have not yet signed a peace treaty to officially end the conflict.

824 Karl Marx, who was Jewish, held a critical view of Judaism and believed that money held a significant role in the religion. He famously stated that "money is the jealous god of Israel."

825 The human heart is an organ that pumps blood throughout the body, it is roughly the size of an adult fist.

826 Kissing someone for one minute has been estimated to burn about 2 calories, but this number can vary depending on various factors such as age, gender, and physical activity.

827 There is no exact physical description of Jesus Christ in the Bible, and what we know about his appearance is mainly based on depictions in art and other cultural references.

828 It is said that none of the 30 engineers on the Titanic survived the sinking of the ship. They reportedly stayed behind to keep the power on in order to ensure that others could escape. This act of selflessness and dedication to duty is often cited as an example of the bravery and sacrifice of the crew of the Titanic.

829 Toilets have played a significant role in improving public health and sanitation over the past 200 years. According to some estimates, the widespread adoption of toilets has added an average of 20 years to the human lifespan by reducing the spread of disease.

830 The budget for the 1997 film "Titanic," directed by James Cameron, was reportedly higher than the cost of building the actual ship. The film, which went on to become one of the highest-grossing films of all time, had an estimated budget of $200 million.

831 Applesauce was the first food consumed by astronauts in space, as it was easy to package and consume in the zero-gravity environment.

832 Light from the sun takes about 8 minutes and 19 seconds to travel to Earth, making it the closest star to our planet.

833 Cats, including domestic cats, share a high degree of genetic similarity with tigers. In fact, studies have shown that cats share approximately 95.6% of their DNA with tigers.

834 Strawberries are unique among fruits in that they have their seeds on the exterior of the fruit rather than on the inside.

Jewish New Year Celebrations.

835 In Judaism, there are four distinct New Year celebrations, each with its own unique significance and customs. Rosh Hashanah, the Jewish New Year, marks the beginning of the civil year and is celebrated in late September or early October. Yom Kippur, the Day of Atonement, falls ten days later and is a time of fasting and repentance. Tu Bishvat, the New Year for Trees, is a holiday celebrated in January or February and is dedicated to the planting of trees in Israel. Finally, there is Shemini Atzeret, a holiday that immediately follows the seven-day festival of Sukkot and is considered a separate New Year for the counting of the agricultural cycle.

836 Koalas are known for their unique sleepy behavior, sleeping up to 20 hours a day. This is a result of their low-energy diet, which consists mainly of eucalyptus leaves. Koalas conserve their energy by sleeping and resting in order to conserve their energy for digestion and other activities.

837 Approximately 10% of the world's population is left-handed. While the exact cause of handedness is still unknown, many scientists believe it is a combination of genetic and environmental factors. Left-handed individuals have been historically marginalized and faced challenges in a world designed for right-handed people, but in recent years, efforts have been made to promote inclusivity and accommodate left-handed individuals.

838 During the Islamic Golden Age, science was highly valued and respected, and scientists were financially compensated at a level that was equivalent to the salaries of contemporary professional athletes.

839 The concept of using contact lenses as a form of vision correction was first recorded by the famous Renaissance inventor and artist, Leonardo Da Vinci, in 1508. He proposed the idea of making lenses from glass that could be placed directly on the eye.

840 Japan is an archipelago comprised of over 6,800 islands, of which four main islands make up most of the country's landmass. These islands are Hokkaido, Honshu, Shikoku, and Kyushu.

841. In 1939, a single lightning strike in Utah resulted in the death of 835 sheep. This was a serious event at the time and gained widespread attention due to the large number of animals affected.

842. The roar of a lion is powerful and can be heard from a distance of up to 8 kilometers. This is due to the strength of their vocal cords and the volume at which they are able to produce sounds.

843. London, one of the world's largest and most influential cities, was founded by the Romans in the first century AD. It was originally known as Londinium and served as a major center of commerce and industry.

844. There is a wealth of diverse life forms living on the human skin, with some estimates suggesting that there are more species of microorganisms on the skin than there are people on the planet.

845. Erika La Tour Eiffel is a woman who claimed to have "married" the Eiffel Tower in 2007 in a symbolic ceremony. This act was part of a larger movement known as Objectum Sexuality, which involves individuals who form romantic and/or sexual relationships with inanimate objects. However, these relationships are not recognized as legally binding by any government.

846. Christmas, a holiday celebrated on December 25th that commemorates the birth of Jesus Christ, was once illegal in the United States. This was due to the holiday being considered an Ancient Pagan Holiday. It was not until 1836 that the holiday was officially recognized and made legal in the United States.

847. Danny Elfman, a well-known American composer and songwriter, composed The Simpsons' famous theme in just two days in 1989. The theme has since become iconic and synonymous with the popular animated television series.

848. Zebras are known to communicate with each other using a variety of vocalizations, including barks, brays, and whinnies, as well as through physical gestures such as nuzzling and touching.

849. In Italy, a men may face arrest for wearing a skirt in public.

850. The Grand Canyon in the United States is one of the most well-known canyons in the world, and is considered to be one of the largest in the world.

851. Russia and the United States are separated by the Bering Strait, which is approximately 55 miles wide at its narrowest point.

852. The Sahara desert, located in northern Africa, is known to be one of the hottest deserts in the world.

853. The Andes mountain range in South America is the longest mountain range in the world, stretching over 7,000 km (4,350 miles) through seven countries.

854. Some species of fish, such as lungfish, have the ability to cough in order to clear their airways.

855. Horses and cows are able to sleep standing up due to a mechanism in their legs called the stay apparatus, which allows them to lock their joints and remain upright without expending energy.

856. Panther is not a distinct species, it is the common name of a black variant of species such as leopard or jaguar.

857. Mars has a lower gravitational pull compared to Earth.

858. Jupiter is the planet with the fastest rotation in the solar system.

859. The nearest star to Earth, Proxima Centauri, is located 4.2 light-years away.

860. The sun's surface temperature is around 10,000 degrees Fahrenheit.

861. The average age of a star is between 1 and 10 billion years.

862. According to predictions, the world's population is expected to reach 9.7 billion by 2050.

863. The oldest known menu dates back to the mid-18th century.

864 It takes a pineapple plant between two to three years to fully mature and produce a fully grown fruit.

865 The human eye is a complex organ that is made up of around 2 million working parts. These parts include the cornea, iris, pupil, lens, and retina, which work together to allow us to see.

866 It is possible to sneeze with your eyes open, although it is difficult to do so and requires a significant effort to keep them open.

867 The most expensive book ever purchased was a copy of Leonardo da Vinci's Codex Leicester, which was sold for $30.8 million in 1994.

868 An avalanche can travel at extremely high speeds, with some reaching up to 80 miles per hour. This is due to the large amount of snow and ice that is rapidly moving down a mountain or hill.

869 The giant panda, also known as just the panda, which is known for its distinctive black and white markings, is actually a bear. It is a member of the bear family, Ursidae. It is a herbivorous species that is native to central China.

870 During a kiss, two people can exchange between 10 million to 1 billion bacteria.

871 Koalas possess fingerprints that are similar to those of humans.

872 Gold has been discovered in various forms on every continent on Earth, making it a highly sought-after precious metal that has been treasured throughout history.

873 If you search for the word "askew" in Google, you may notice that the content appears to tilt slightly to the right, adding a playful touch to the search experience.

874 Michael Phelps, the most decorated Olympian of all time, faced challenges in his youth as he was bullied for his unusual appearance, including his long arms and big ears. However, he persevered and went on to achieve great success in the world of swimming.

875 Buddhism has a strong global following, with an estimated 7 million followers residing outside of Asia. This shows that the religion and its teachings have transcended cultural and geographical boundaries to gain a widespread appeal.

876 The formation of memories plays an essential role in shaping our identity and understanding of the world. Researchers have discovered that every time we form a memory, new connections are formed in the brain. This demonstrates the tremendous plasticity of the human brain and its ability to constantly adapt and grow.

877 Brazil is home to a large number of airports, second only to the United States. This reflects the country's significance as a hub for regional and international air travel, providing convenient access for millions of travelers every year.

878 Bolivia boasts an impressive linguistic diversity, with 37 official languages recognized by the government.

879 The melting properties of mozzarella cheese make it the ideal topping for pizza, according to a 2014 study. The cheese's ability to melt evenly and consistently, combined with its mild and versatile flavor, make it a popular choice among pizza enthusiasts.

880 The Bill and Melinda Gates Foundation is a major player in global health, dedicating a substantial portion of its resources to improving health outcomes around the world. In many cases, the Foundation's yearly spending on global health exceeds that of the World Health Organization, a specialized agency of the United Nations.

881 The five cities in the United States with the worst air pollution are all located in California.

882 A recent study suggests that a lack of physical activity is causing as many deaths globally as smoking. This highlights the critical role that exercise plays in maintaining good health and the need for individuals to prioritize physical activity in their daily lives.

883. The Golden Gate Bridge, one of the most recognizable landmarks in the United States, attracts millions of visitors each year. Unfortunately, it also serves as a site for suicide, with an average of one person jumping from the bridge every two weeks.

884. In Hawaii, owning a pet hamster is illegal. This law is in place to protect both the pet and the environment, as hamsters have been known to cause damage to the local ecosystem.

885. It is estimated that 160,000 American children miss school every day due to fears of bullying. This is a major problem that needs to be addressed by educators, parents, and community leaders.

886. The aroma of chocolate has been found to increase theta brain waves, which in turn promotes relaxation. This is just one of the many benefits that people can enjoy by consuming chocolate, which has long been considered a comfort food.

887. In Brazil, voting is mandatory by law. This means that citizens are required to participate in the electoral process and make their voices heard in the democratic process.

888. Japan is home to a number of "cat islands," where cats outnumber people. These places have become popular tourist destinations and are known for their friendly and relaxed atmosphere.

889. The James Webb Space Telescope is capable of observing the universe from its earliest days, allowing scientists to see back in time and gain a better understanding of the evolution of the cosmos.

890. The popular search engine, Google, was originally named "Backrub." However, the company changed its name to Google, which has since become synonymous with online search and information.

891. The Harry Potter book series has been translated into over 70 different languages, making it accessible to millions of readers around the world.

892 According to some experts, laughing 100 times is the equivalent of 15 minutes of exercise on a stationary bicycle.

893 Cars are produced at a rate of approximately 165,000 per day. The exact number may fluctuate, but this is a general estimate.

894 There are over 100 different types of cancers, each affecting different areas of the body and requiring different treatments. Cancer is a complex and diverse group of diseases, making it a challenge for medical professionals.

895 Canada is home to an exceptional number of lakes, with more than all of the world's lakes combined. This abundance of fresh water is a defining characteristic of the country and contributes to its natural beauty and diverse ecosystem.

896 Brazil has been the leading producer of coffee for the past 150 years. The country's favorable climate, dedicated coffee-growing communities, and government support have all helped to establish Brazil as the largest coffee producer in the world.

897 In Italy, it is considered unlucky to place bread upside down, either on a table or in a basket. This cultural belief dates back centuries and is still observed by many people in Italy today.

898 Relative to their body size, barnacles have the largest penises in the animal kingdom. This unique characteristic has been the subject of scientific study and is considered a remarkable adaptation for these creatures.

899 Sleeping less than seven hours per night has been linked to a reduction in life expectancy. Adequate sleep is essential for maintaining physical and mental health, and a lack of sleep can lead to a variety of negative health consequences.

900 Every minute, an estimated two million searches are performed on Google.

901 Humans are unique among animals in that we are the only species confirmed to shed tears as a result of our emotions.

Olympic gold medals are not made of pure gold

902 Olympic gold medals may have the word "gold" in their name, but they are actually composed of very little pure gold. In fact, the gold content of an Olympic gold medal is only 1.34%. The majority of the medal is made up of other metals, including silver and copper. Despite this, Olympic gold medals remain some of the most prized and coveted awards in the world.

903 Although they are named after the country, Brazil are not actually the primary exporter of Brazil nuts. Instead, the largest exporter of Brazil nuts is Bolivia.

904 The circulatory system of a human body is incredibly efficient, with red blood cells completing a full circuit in an impressive 30 seconds.

905 In Brazil, 92% of newly sold vehicles run on ethanol fuel, which is derived from sugar cane crops.

906 Every two seconds, there is someone in the United States who requires a blood transfusion.

907 Ravens in captive environments have demonstrated an ability to develop stronger language skills than parrots, with some studies showing that they can mimic human speech more accurately.

908 In Germany, it is considered a positive omen when a black cat crosses your path from right to left. This superstition has been a part of German culture for centuries and is still held by many people today.

909 Eggplants are scientifically classified as berries due to their characteristic fleshy fruit and seeds surrounded by a pulpy flesh. While they may not resemble the traditional definition of a berry, their classification as such is based on scientific criteria.

910 In a unique turn of events, Brazil once attempted to sell an aircraft carrier on eBay, showcasing its willingness to embrace technology in unexpected ways.103

911. There are currently 1 billion cars in use on Earth, providing a means of transportation for people all around the world.

912. Tragically, over 20,000 people die from cancer every day, making it one of the leading causes of death globally.

913. Canada is known for its vast geography and is considered to be the second largest country in the world by total area.

914. "Tinku" is a traditional festival in Bolivia that involves people engaging in physical fights with each other, sometimes for a duration of 2-3 days.

915. Only female mosquitoes drink blood. Males feed on nectar and other plant-based sources of carbohydrates. Female mosquitoes need the protein and other nutrients found in blood to produce and lay their eggs.

916. The concept of a "left brain/right brain divide" refers to the idea that the two hemispheres of the brain have distinct and separate functions. However, this idea is a myth. In reality, the two hemispheres work together in a dynamic and integrated manner, constantly communicating and collaborating with each other to achieve various cognitive tasks.

917. One pint of donated blood can have a powerful impact on saving lives. According to the American Red Cross, one pint of blood can help save up to three lives, as it can be separated into its components (red cells, plasma, and platelets) and used to treat different medical conditions. Donating blood is a simple yet meaningful act that can make a big difference.

918. Benjamin Franklin, one of the founding fathers of the United States, had a limited formal education. He only attended school until the age of 10, after which he became a self-taught man and pursued his interests in reading, writing, and scientific experimentation. Despite his lack of formal education, Franklin went on to become one of the most accomplished individuals of his time.

919. When it comes to purchasing printer ink, it may surprise some consumers to learnthat black ink for HP printers can be more expensive than blood.

Did you know?

920 Volkswagen is a parent company that owns several well-known automotive brands, including Bentley, Bugatti, Lamborghini, Audi, Ducati, and Porsche. These brands operate independently but under the umbrella of the Volkswagen Group.

921 In the United Kingdom, the monarch is considered the owner of all unmarked marine life in the country's waters, including dolphins. However, this is a largely symbolic designation and the monarch has no practical control over the dolphins.

922 The adult human body is equipped with an extensive network of blood vessels, numbering approximately 100,000 miles in length. This complex system of vessels is responsible for carrying blood, oxygen, and other essential nutrients to all parts of the body.

923 China is a big global provider of Bibles, with a large number of Bibles being manufactured and distributed in the country.

924 At the time of his swearing-in ceremony as the first President of the United States in 1789, George Washington had lost many of his teeth and was left with only one remaining. Despite this, he went on to serve two terms as President and is widely considered one of the country's founding fathers.

925 Goosebumps are a physical response that occurs when a small muscle called the arrector pili muscle contracts. This contraction causes the hair on the skin to stand up, creating the sensation and appearance of goosebumps.

926 The Golden Gate Bridge, located in San Francisco, California, is unfortunately known for being the location of a high number of suicides. As a result, the bridge has implemented various measures aimed at preventing suicide and providing support to those in need.

927 In the year 1924, a significant portion of the automobiles globally were manufactured by the Ford Motor Company. This company's popularity and widespread use of their vehicles at the time contributed to this statistic.

928 Mosquitoes are known to have a preference for blood type "O".

929 Canada is renowned for being a highly educated nation, with over half of its population holding college degrees. This has contributed to the country's well-developed and highly skilled workforce.

930 School shootings have been a growing concern globally, and research shows that 75% of these incidents are related to bullying and harassment. It is crucial that measures are taken to address these issues in schools, to ensure the safety and well-being of students and staff.

931 Bill Gates is one of the world's wealthiest individuals, with a net worth estimated at over $100 billion. If he were to spend $1 million every day, it would take him 218 years to exhaust his entire fortune. This staggering amount of wealth illustrates the vast disparity between the rich and poor, and the need for equal distribution of resources and opportunities.

932 The name "Google" is one of the most recognizable brand names in the world, but it was actually chosen by accident. The founders of the company initially intended to call it "Googol," which is a mathematical term for the number represented by 1 followed by 100 zeros. However, they mistakenly misspelled the word as "Google," and the name stuck. This serves as a reminder that sometimes, the best things in life are the result of happy accidents.

933 The Bible is considered one of the most widely purchased and read books in history, often referred to as the best-selling book of all time.

934 During World War I, a significant number of French soldiers lost their lives, surpassing the number of American casualties throughout the history of the United States.

935 Sea cucumbers are unique creatures that feed by using their feet to gather food particles from the ocean floor.

936 Hippopotomonstrosesquippedaliophobia is a term used to describe the fear of long words, a common phobia among many individuals.

937 The James Webb Space Telescope is named after James E. Webb, who served as the second administrator of NASA during his career. The telescope is designed to further our understanding of the universe and the formation of galaxies, stars, and planetary systems.

938 The United States Senate has a rule, referred to as Rule XIX, which restricts senators from utilizing language or behavior that is disrespectful or insulting towards their colleagues. This is to maintain a level of professionalism and decorum within the Senate chamber.

939 On August 10, 1984, the movie "Red Dawn" was released in theaters and marked a milestone in film history. It was the first movie to be given a PG-13 rating by the Motion Picture Association of America, indicating that it contained material that may be inappropriate for children under the age of 13 but still acceptable for those over the age. This rating system provided a clearer guideline for parents and movie-goers.

940 The word "publicly" is widely known for being misspelled, and it is often cited as one of the most commonly misspelled words in the English language. Despite its simplicity, the spelling of "publicly" is frequently confused with other similar words, leading to its high frequency of misspelling.

941 The first item ever sold on eBay was a broken laser pointer, marking the beginning of the online marketplace's success. Since then, eBay has grown into one of the largest e-commerce platforms in the world, offering a wide variety of goods for sale.

942 Caribbean sperm whales have a unique way of communicating with each other, with distinct vocal patterns that are almost like their own individual accents. Scientists have studied these vocalizations and found that each whale has a distinct sound that is recognizable to other whales in their pod.

943 A group of clowns is sometimes referred to as a "giggle." This term is used to describe a collection of performers who specialize in entertaining audiences through comedic skits, physical humor, and other forms of clowning.

944 Your hair may contain traces of gold, as this precious metal is present in trace amounts in the earth's crust. While the amount of gold in hair is negligible, it is still a fascinating fact that this metal can be found in this unlikely location.

945 The term "butt" was once used as a unit of measurement for wine casks. A butt is equivalent to approximately two hogsheads, or 108 gallons. This unit of measurement is now considered obsolete and is no longer in common use.

946 Kea parrots are known for producing warbles, trill-like sounds, when they are in a good mood. These birds are highly intelligent and are known for their playful and curious nature, which can often result in them making these cheerful vocalizations.

947 The Scottish pop band known as The Bay City Rollers selected their name in a unique way. They chose the name after randomly sticking a pin in a map of the United States and wherever it landed, that became the name of the band. In this case, the pin landed on the city of Bay City, Michigan.

948 The NASA Vehicle Assembly Building in Florida is a massive structure and is so large that it even has its own microclimate. The building is so tall that it affects the surrounding air pressure, creating its own weather patterns, including wind and temperature fluctuations.

949 In the world of bats, female bats have a unique way of giving birth. They hang upside down while giving birth, which is made possible by the strong muscles in their legs. This allows them to have their offspring safely suspended from the roost while they give birth.

950 The Wife Carrying World Championships is an annual event held in Finland, where contestants compete in a race while carrying their wives. The winner of the race receives a prize that is the weight of their wife in beer. This competition is a lighthearted event and is meant to be a fun and playful celebration.

951 Yawning has long been believed to be a way of communicating tiredness or boredom, but recent research has shown that it may also serve a more important function. It has been discovered that yawning helps to cool the brain, by increasing the flow of blood and oxygen to the brain, which helps regulate its temperature.

952 Swimming the full length of the Mississippi River is a significant challenge that requires dedication and strength. It is estimated that it would take approximately 68 days to swim the entire length of the river, from its source in Minnesota to its mouth in Louisiana.

953 The creator of the Pringles can, Fredric Baur, was so proud of his invention that he requested to be buried in one of the cans. This unique request was fulfilled, and he was interred in a Pringles can after his passing.

954 Penguins have a fascinating history and were once much larger than they are today. Fossil evidence suggests that penguins used to be six feet tall, making them considerably larger than the penguins we see today. These large penguins lived millions of years ago and have since evolved into the smaller penguins that we are familiar with today.

955 An apple is known for its durability and can last for up to 10 months if stored properly. This is due to the apple's natural defense mechanisms, which slow down the process of decay, allowing it to last for a relatively long time.

956 In 1943, Richard James, a mechanical engineer, was working on developing springs for the US Navy when he accidentally dropped one and watched it "walk" down a staircase. This led to the creation of the Slinky, one of the most popular toys in history.

957 For a period of 200 years, the letter Z was not used in the English alphabet. This was due to the influence of Latin and Greek languages, which did not have the letter Z. Eventually, the letter was reinstated, and it is now a common letter used in the English language.

958 A professional coffee taster, whose job was to sample and evaluate coffee, insured his tongue for a whopping £10 million. This was because his tongue was considered a valuable asset to the coffee industry and an insurance policy protected his livelihood.

959 When we listen to music that we enjoy, our brain releases dopamine, a chemical associated with pleasure and reward. This release can cause physical sensations, such as chills or goosebumps, as our bodies respond to the pleasurable experience.

960 Pumpkin growers have created some truly massive pumpkins, with the current world record weighing over 2,000 pounds. This is heavier than many sports cars.

961 Despite being one of the most iconic and recognizable figures in the entertainment industry, country singer Dolly Parton once lost a lookalike contest.

962 Referees play an important role in the NFL, and their contributions are recognized with a Super Bowl ring. These rings are awarded to all members of the winning team, including referees, as a symbol of their victory.

963 Armando, a Belgian racing pigeon, is considered one of the greatest racing pigeons of all time and was sold for a staggering $1.4 million.

964. There is a correlation between hairiness and higher intelligence quotient (IQ). However, it is important to note that this correlation does not necessarily mean that being hairy causes higher IQ or vice versa.

965. Pablo Picasso was a suspect in the theft of the Mona Lisa from the Louvre in 1911. He was eventually cleared of any involvement in the crime.

966. Horseshoe crabs have numerous tiny eyes on their bodies that help them detect light and navigate their environment.

967. Hawaiian pizza is not actually from Hawaii, but was instead invented in Canada by a Greek restaurateur.

968. The world's longest fingernails on a single hand were over two feet in length and were achieved by Lee Redmond from the United States.

969. Cleopatra was of Greek descent and was a member of the Ptolemaic dynasty, which ruled Egypt at the time.

970. Tug-of-war was once considered an Olympic discipline and was part of the Olympic Games from 1900 to 1920.

971. The Althing, Iceland's parliament, is considered the oldest continuously functioning parliamentary institution in the world, with roots dating back to the 10th century.

972. The Eiffel Tower, was initially intended for the city of Barcelona, Spain as a temporary structure for the 1889 Universal Exposition, but was eventually built in Paris due to the more favorable conditions for its construction.

973. The letter "J" is actually the most recent addition to the modern English alphabet, and its use as a separate letter is relatively recent, only becoming common in the 17th century. Prior to that, it was typically used as a variation of "I."

974. The "ManhattAnt" is a species of ant that is found exclusively in New York City and is believed to have originated from South America.

975 Some regions in Canada, particularly those close to the Hudson Bay, have lower gravity compared to other parts of the world due to the presence of a large mass of land that is pulling down on the Earth's crust.

976 A golf ball typically travels farther during the summer than it does in the winter due to a number of factors, including warmer air temperatures and increased air pressure, which can affect the ball's trajectory and distance.

977 Golf, the sport that involves hitting a small ball into a hole with a club, was the first sport to be played on the moon. This was accomplished by astronaut Alan Shepard in 1971 during the Apollo 14 mission.

978 The world's largest waterfall, the Mero Falls, is located in the Atlantic Ocean and is believed to be underwater. This is due to the sheer size of the waterfall and the fact that it is located on the ocean floor.

979 Putting sugar on a cut will not make it heal faster. This is a common misconception, but in reality, sugar can actually slow down the healing process by attracting bacteria and impeding the body's natural immune response.

980 It took four centuries for women to gain the right to play golf. This was a long and arduous journey, marked by many challenges and obstacles, but ultimately, women were able to break down barriers and participate in this popular sport.

981 Producing one pound of chocolate requires the use of approximately 400 cocoa beans. This is a labor-intensive process that involves the cultivation and harvesting of the beans, followed by roasting, grinding, and finally, conching.

982 A solar eclipse played a surprising role in ending a six-year war that took place in 585 BCE.

983 A dime, a commonly used coin in the United States, has 118 ridges around its circumference. These ridges help to differentiate it from other coins and provide grip for easier handling.

984 The small dot above the letter "i" in the alphabet is known as a tittle. This tiny mark is an important part of written language and helps to distinguish between letters that are similar in appearance.

985 In the past, soccer balls were also used for playing basketball. However, as the popularity of basketball grew, specialized balls were developed to better suit the needs of the game.

986 Sailors working for the Royal Navy must obtain special permission to grow a beard. This is because beards were once seen as a safety hazard, as they could become tangled in ropes or machinery. Today, however, beards are allowed with certain restrictions.

987 Every second, McDonald's sells 75 burgers worldwide. This is a testament to the popularity and widespread reach of this fast-food giant, which serves millions of people every day.

988 Sleeping on your stomach has been linked to having more vivid and potentially strange or scary dreams. This is because this position can cause your neck to twist, leading to changes in blood flow and brain activity that may affect your dreaming.

989 In space, it is not necessary to use welding materials to fuse two metals, as they can bond on their own due to the lack of gravity and atmospheric pressure. This is known as cold welding.

990 Chinese checkers, a popular board game, was actually invented in Germany.

991: Octavia E. Butler, a well-known writer, had a humble start to her career as a potato chip inspector.

992: Did you know that a day in the age of dinosaurs was just 23 hours long? This was because the speed of the Earth's rotation changes over time.

993: In 1897, the Indiana state legislature attempted to pass a bill that would have redefined the value of pi as 3.2. However, this bill was not passed.

994: The first Macy's Thanksgiving Day Parade, held in 1924, featured exotic animals such as lions, camels, and elephants from the Central Park Zoo.

995: Foreign Accent Syndrome is a rare medical condition that occurs as a side effect of brain trauma. Patients affected by this syndrome speak their native language with a foreign accent.

996: Sharks have existed on our planet for over 400 million years, far predating the appearance of trees. This longevity speaks to their incredible adaptability and resilience, and underscores their importance as a key species in our planet's ecosystem.

997: Eighteen percent of Americans claim to have had some form of paranormal experience, such as seeing or feeling the presence of a ghost. Whether or not these experiences are real, they remain a fascinating aspect of our cultural landscape and continue to captivate the imagination of people around the world.

998: In Queensland, Australia, owning a pet rabbit is illegal unless one is a licensed magician. This bizarre law reflects the unique culture and laws of this region, and highlights the importance of researching local regulations before adopting a pet.

999: The city of Melbourne took an innovative approach by assigning email addresses to some of its trees. This was done so residents could report any issues, however, the trees ended up receiving love letters instead.

1000: Wrestling is widely considered as the earliest form of sport as we know it today. It is believed to have originated in Greece in 776 BC

1001 Marie Curie remains the only individual in history to have won Nobel Prizes in two separate scientific fields. This remarkable achievement solidifies her legacy as one of the most influential scientists of all time.

1002 Queen Elizabeth II has had a lifelong love for corgis and has owned over 30 of these lovable dogs throughout her reign. Her affection for these dogs has endeared her to many people around the world and made her a beloved figure in pop culture.

BONUS

1003 Alice in Wonderland, a beloved children's story written by Lewis Carroll, has been banned in certain parts of China due to its perceived subversion of cultural and societal norms. Despite this, it remains a popular and enduring tale that has captured the imagination of readers for generations.

1004 President Thomas Jefferson was known for his aversion to formal affairs, and was known to greet foreign dignitaries in his pajamas on occasion. This eccentric behavior was a reflection of his unique personality and his commitment to maintaining a relaxed and informal atmosphere in his personal life.

1005 Throughout her sixty-three-year reign, Queen Victoria faced numerous challenges, including eight assassination attempts. Despite these threats to her safety, she remained a beloved and revered figure, and her reign was characterized by stability and prosperity.

1006 A double rainbow is a stunning meteorological phenomenon that occurs when sunlight is reflected twice inside a raindrop. The result is a brilliant display of colors that can be seen across the sky.

1007 Sebastian Vettel, a renowned Formula One driver, is known to keep lucky coins in his racing boots for good luck.

1008 Michael Phelps, a retired American swimmer, has won a record-breaking number of Olympic gold medals, surpassing the total number of Olympic golds won by Mexico.

1009 According to records, the first recorded diving championship in the United Kingdom took place in 1889.

1010 The World's Sports Encyclopedia states that there are over 8000 known sports across the world.

1011 Modern swimsuits have seen great advancements in their design and technology, with some suits now being more hydrodynamic in water than human skin.

1012 The diameter of a basketball hoop used to be nearly double the size of a basketball, but it has since been standardized to its current size.

1013 The length of the grass at Wimbledon has changed over the years. In 1949, a snake bite incident involving an English player resulted in the decision to keep the grass shorter.

1014 While many parts of the body have the ability to heal, human teeth are an exception. They are the only part of the body that cannot heal themselves.

1015 Blue whales are known for having the largest hearts of any living species. Their heartbeats can be heard from over two miles away, which is a testament to their size.

1016 Humans and chimpanzees have a similar number of hair follicles, which is interesting considering their evolutionary differences. This commonality sheds light on the shared ancestry of these two species.

1017 In the United States, cats are a popular choice for pet ownership. In fact, they are considered to be the most popular pets in America.

1018 Unfortunately, in China, nearly four million cats are consumed as a delicacy each year.

1019 Research has shown that owning a cat can have numerous health benefits, including reducing the risk of heart attacks and strokes by more than one-third.

1020 Ancient Egyptians had a deep reverence for cats, and upon the death of a beloved feline, it was customary for them to shave their eyebrows as a sign of mourning.

1021 Chimpanzees possess the ability to recognize individual members of their group through visual examination of their hindquarters. This is an example of the remarkable cognitive and social skills that these primates possess.

1022 In China, a small portion of the population still resides in cave dwellings. Reports indicate that over 35 million people live in these traditional homes, often in rural and remote areas of the country. This form of housing is a result of both cultural tradition and economic necessity, and while it may seem primitive to some, it provides a unique and sustainable way of life for those who choose it.

1023 In the wild, chimpanzees have been observed to self-medicate by using certain plants as remedies for illnesses and injuries. This behavior highlights their innate understanding of the properties of their environment and their ability to use it to their advantage.

1024 The Earth has a diameter of about 12,742 kilometers (7,918 miles), and its core, which is located at the center, has a radius of about 3,485 kilometers (2,165 miles). If you were to dig a hole all the way through the Earth and jump in, it would take you approximately 42 minutes to reach the center, assuming there is no air resistance and you are falling freely under the force of gravity.

1025 The first recorded instance of a speeding fine occurred in 1896 in the United Kingdom. A motorist named Walter Arnold was caught driving at the breakneck speed of 8 miles per hour in a 2-mile per hour zone, and was subsequently fined one shilling by a police officer.

1026 Microraptor is a genus of small, feathered theropod dinosaurs that lived in the Early Cretaceous period, about 120 million years ago. They were first discovered in China in 2000 and are known for their small size, with some species measuring only about 1 meter (3.3 feet) in length.

1027 The Moon is tidally locked with Earth, which means that it takes the same amount of time to rotate on its axis as it does to orbit around Earth. As a result, we always see the same side of the Moon facing us. The side of the Moon that we can see is known as the near side, while the side that is always facing away from us is called the far side or the "dark side" of the Moon (although it is not always dark; it receives sunlight just like the near side). Because the Moon's rotation and revolution periods are synchronized, the far side of the Moon has only been seen by a few spacecraft and astronauts who have orbited or landed on it, but it has never been seen directly from Earth.

1028 Pringles have an official shape that is recognizable around the world. They are known for their distinctive hyperbolic paraboloid shape, which is sometimes described as a "saddle shape" or a "duckbill" shape. This unique shape is designed to prevent the chips from breaking and to stack more efficiently in the can.

1029 A newborn baby's body is made up of a large percentage of water. According to various sources, a newborn baby's body is typically composed of around 75% water. This is because babies have a higher water content than adults due to a number of factors, including their higher metabolic rate, higher surface area-to-mass ratio, and immature kidneys which require more water to eliminate waste products.

1030 During the 17th century, tulips were more valuable than gold in the Netherlands. This period of time is known as the "tulip mania" or "tulip craze," which occurred in the Dutch Golden Age, a time when the Netherlands was the world's leading economic power. During this period, tulips became a status symbol and a luxury item, especially among the wealthy.

1031 It is possible for tonsils to grow back. Tonsils are a pair of small, soft tissue masses located at the back of the throat, and they play a role in the body's immune system by helping to filter out harmful bacteria and viruses. In some cases, people who have had their tonsils surgically removed may experience regrowth of the tonsil tissue. This is more likely to occur in children, and may be due to the fact that the tonsil tissue was not completely removed during the initial surgery.

1032 Santa Claus has an official pilot's license. In the United States, the Federal Aviation Administration (FAA) issues "special airworthiness certificates" to aircraft that are not used for traditional transportation purposes, such as balloons, gliders, and even sleighs used for commercial purposes. In the case of Santa Claus, the FAA has issued him a special airworthiness certificate, allowing him to operate his sleigh and reindeer on Christmas Eve without having to comply with the standard aviation regulations. The certificate is officially known as a "Santa Claus Certificate of Airworthiness" and is signed by the FAA Administrator.

CONCLUSION

In conclusion, we hope this book has provided a captivating and educational journey through a collection of fascinating and unusual facts. The diverse range of topics covered, from science and history to culture and nature, highlights the incredible complexity and beauty of our world.

The book has demonstrated that there is always more to discover and learn, even about the most well-known topics. These interesting facts serve as a reminder of the boundless wonder and curiosity that surrounds us, and the importance of constantly seeking out new knowledge and experiences. Whether you are a lifelong learner or just seeking to expand your knowledge, we hope this book has something to offer for everyone.

"We hope you had a great time reading our book. If you found it enjoyable and informative, we would greatly appreciate it if you could leave a review on Amazon. Your kind words will help others discover and benefit from this book as well."

Printed in Great Britain
by Amazon